THE MYSTERY OF FAITH
THE MINISTERS
OF MUSIC

Lawrence J. Johnson

Illustrations by Marion C. Honors, CSJ

National Association of Pastoral Musicians
Washington, DC

Contents

Introduction

In an address delivered several years ago at the first national meeting of the National Association of Pastoral Musicians Archbishop Rembert Weakland summoned pastoral musicians to develop their musical talents, liturgical knowledge and sensitivity, and to deepen their own personal prayer life. The phenomenal success of the NPM with its diocesan chapters, national and regional meetings, and various publications, is but one sign that musicians, in ever increasing numbers, are responding to the Archbishop's challenge. It is apparent that those who share in the ministry of music are not, by and large, a complacent lot, but rather an exuberant, highly dedicated group of men and women eager to go beyond functional, albeit important, details to come to grips with such personal questions as "who are we and what are we about?". It is only through such questioning and the insights it engenders that true growth in ministry is nourished, that technical craftsmanship is transcended and transformed into service. This volume is designed to assist all who serve the community's musical prayer in their continuing quest to be what they are. Though it may be used for other purposes, the book is primarily intended to serve as a springboard for common, shared reflection on occasions when pastoral musicians come together to articulate their own experiences of what it means to be artists who unselfishly and lovingly channel their musical gifts on behalf of a community at prayer.

Modeled after the BCL-FDLC publication *The Mystery of Faith*, this source book considers the various expressions of the Church's ministry of music, e.g. assembly, presider, deacon, cantor, choir, etc. It does so first by sketching the historical background for each form of service. Admittedly, the definitive and comprehensive history of music in the Roman liturgy remains to be written. Much detailed research, the very marrow of scholarly inquiry, is still to be initiated. Yet certain outlines are discernible. Notwithstanding their often fragmentary nature, they can offer the pastoral musician a sense of continuity with and an appreciation for the past. Pertinent sections of various official documents are then provided. Though ecclesiastical directives wisely refrain from legislating artistic matters, they rightly delineate the general function of the musical arts and the role of various ministers of music in liturgical celebration. Pastoral musicians can always profit from going to the written "sources" describing their ministries. A short reflection followed by several suggested questions for discussion follows. By design both are seminal rather than exhaustive. Finally, there is a bibliography for further reading. To the many authors whose books and articles are listed a word of appreciation is due for numerous and unacknowledged insights into what it means to be a pastoral musician in the Church today.

This book would not have been possible without the support and assistance of many people. It was suggested by Fr. Virgil Funk. The manuscript was read and invaluable suggestions were made by Linus M. Ellis III and J. Michael McMahon who together with Sr. Marilyn Winter, O.P., Linda Raineri, and Michael Helman helped formulate questions for discussion. I am especially indebted to my wife, Marlene Winter-Johnson, not only for a critical reading of the text but also for her patient understanding.

1
Assembly

1

Assembly

Historical Background

Although the New Testament and other early sources leave no doubt that the apostolic and subapostolic Church was a singing community, we know relatively little as to the exact details of the assembly's musical role. The literary evidence is fragmentary and not concerned with technical details. Pliny the Younger, in a letter written to the Emperor Trajan about 112, reports that the Christians had been accustomed "to gather before dawn on a fixed day and to sing a hymn (*carmen*) to Christ as if to a god . . . ."[1] According to some scholars this assembly was for the celebration of baptism, and the hymn may well have been a baptismal profession of faith. Justin, writing in Rome about the year 150, calls special attention to the "Amen" given by the people as they assented to the eucharistic prayer, and yet he does not indicate the manner in which this response was given.[2] In Africa, Tertullian (c.160-c.220) remarks that "the scriptures are read, the psalms are sung, and sermons are preached."[3] Psalmody, hymnody, and other forms of chant were undoubtedly simple in melody, in all probability resembling song-speech. In fact, many believe that the distinction between singing and reciting liturgical texts was, in the early days of the Church, less defined than it is today. Possibly the size of the assembly, its place of gathering, and the nature of the celebration would have determined the precise manner of rendering liturgical texts.

3

It was only during the fourth and fifth centuries, a period characterized by a growth of liturgical forms and practices, that references to the singing of the assembly appear with increasing frequency. This is especially true for the chanting of the psalms and hymns at services such as vigils, morning prayer, and evening prayer. In a letter to the people of Caesaria, St. Basil the Great (c.330-379) says: "The people come early after nightfall to the house of prayer . . . . And now, divided into two parts, they chant antiphonally . . . ."[4] And Egeria, probably a Spanish nun, in her description of a journey to the holy places in the East at the end of the fourth century, relates that monks, virgins, priests, and laics participated in the daily offices by singing hymns and responses to the psalms.[5] But even at this time there is little explicit evidence regarding details of the assembly's sung participation during the eucharistic celebration. Nevertheless, St. Augustine (354-430) in Africa surely reflects a tradition when he remarks: "Apart from those moments when the scriptures are being read or a sermon is preached, when the bishop is praying aloud or the deacon is speaking the intention of the litany of community prayer, is there any time when the faithful assembled are not singing? Truly I see nothing better, more useful or more holy that they could do."[6] As regards Rome, we know few musical details till the pontificate of St. Gregory the Great (590-604) when the people, at times with the assisting clergy, sang the Kyrie, perhaps the Gloria, and the Sanctus. At the end of the seventh century the Agnus Dei, added to the Mass to accompany the breaking of the eucharistic bread, was also sung by the people. The assembly would also have responded in a type of song to whatever texts may have been chanted by the presider and to those rendered by the psalmist or cantor.

"To sing with one voice" is a motif which constantly occurs in the patristic references to the song of the assembly.[7] Just as the breaking and reception of the eucharistic bread are a sign that all who partake become one body in Christ, so singing is to be a vehicle for expressing this same unity of hearts and minds. St. Basil (c.330-379), for example, speaks of psalmody as "a bond of unity harmoniously drawing people to the symphony of one choir."[8] This unity even extends beyond the members of the assembly on earth. According to the Fathers, it is through singing that the faithful also join the angels in heaven and all creation in offering praise to God. In the words of St. John Chrysostom (c.345-407), "the psalms which occurred just now in the office blended all voices together, and caused one single full harmonious chant to arise; young and old, rich and poor, women and men, slaves and free, all sang one single melody . . . . together we make up a single choir in perfect equality of rights and of expression whereby earth imitates heaven."[9] At times the people even expressed their unity by joining hands while singing, a practice related by Acadius of Constantinople in 561.[10]

During the fourth and fifth centuries the spiritual bond achieved and expressed through common song was weakened by the attacks of a few somewhat isolated voices objecting to the active participation of women in the liturgy. The *Didascalia of the Three Hundred Eighteen Fathers*, dated about 375, says: "Women are ordered not to speak in church, not even softly, nor may they sing along or take part in the responses, but they should be silent and pray to God."[11] Sharing this opinion was St. Isidore of Pelusium (d.c.450). He admitted the possibility that women were permitted to sing within the liturgy in the earliest days of the Church, but this was only to prevent them from gossiping.[12] This restriction, found also among other writers, seems to have originated in opposition to the practice of certain heterdox groups which established female choirs to sing during worship services. Reaction against certain pagan cults of the dead which employed female singers may also have contributed to this exclusion of women from singing in the assembly. And yet the prohibition was far from universal. St. Ambrose (c.339-397), while recalling St. Paul's injunction against women speaking in the assembly (I Cor 14:34), points out that women "also do well to sing the psalms: it is sweet for every age and suitable for either sex . . . and it is a great bond of unity when all the people raise their voices in one chorus."[13] While the exclusion of women from the singing assembly was more local than general, to some degree it may have contributed to the disintegration of the assembly's musical participation at Mass. We find what appears to be the first indication of this at Rome toward the end of the seventh century.

The earliest complete description of the Roman Mass, one celebrated by the pope, is found in Roman Ordo I, a document written shortly after 701.[14] What is noteworthy is that the Ordo makes no explicit reference to singing by the assembly. Consequently some believe that by the end of the seventh century the assembly no longer participated in song at the papal Mass. Yet it may also be true that the scribe merely was not interested in portraying all the details of the celebration. At any rate, Ordo I offers an excellent point of departure for tracing the history of the assembly's sung participation in the Roman Mass. It also evidences the growing appropriation of the assembly's musical role by a select group of singers.

The celebration began with a schola cantorum singing a chant to accompany the procession of the ministers. It is apparently the schola alone which sang the Kyrie, although at the time of Pope Gregory the Great (590-604) this litany was led by the clergy with the people responding.[15] After the Kyrie the pope turned toward the people and intoned the Gloria, but the Ordo says nothing specific regarding the singers of this hymn. Some believe that the Gloria was from the beginning a song of the people since its oldest notated melodies are syllabic in style. Perhaps it remained so at this time since the bishop turned toward the assembly as he began the hymn. It may also be true that this rubric is merely a relic from a former practice. Many subsequent accounts refer to the chorus, i.e. the clergy assisting the bishop, as singing the Gloria, although a few non-Roman sources still speak of this hymn as a song of the people.[16]

The liturgy of the word began with a scripture reading followed by a psalm sung by the soloist. Although the musical genre of responsorial psalmody would presume the whole assembly responding after each of the verses, this is not mentioned. Perhaps the response was given by the schola. On appropriate days the Alleluia followed. While in the East the Alleluia was sung by the people as a refrain to the cantor's psalmody, in the West it was a neumatic solo chant, one which in time came to be repeated after the soloist by the schola. On penitential days the Alleluia was replaced by a tract which was sung straight through by the soloist alone. Ordo I does not mention the Creed since this entered the liturgy at Rome only in 1014. In ninth century France, however, all sang the profession of faith. This practice differed from that of the East where a simple recitation was the rule. In time the long text of the Creed posed a problem in the West, one which admitted various solutions: the people singing the Apostles' Creed; the assembly singing a vernacular profession of faith after the Nicene Creed; the singing of the creed by the assisting clerics.[17]

The schola began the liturgy of the eucharist by singing a psalm to accompany the procession with the gifts. The Sanctus was sung by the assisting clergy, although as late as the sixth century it was sung by the people, a custom continued outside the Pontifical Mass even after the time of Ordo I.[18] Although Ordo I assigns the Agnus Dei to the schola, it was initially chanted by the people and the clergy. And yet it is possible that, in the papal Mass, the schola merely intoned the chant, with the clergy and people giving the response as was customary in France during succeeding centuries. Finally it was the schola which chanted the psalm during the communion procession.

Ordo I witnesses a trend which would accelerate in centuries to follow as clergy and schola increasingly appropriated the chants of the people. Although efforts to maintain or restore the traditional song of the assembly were undertaken outside Rome and especially in the Carolingian empire, the musical exclusion of the people from the Mass had in most areas been completed by the eleventh and twelfth centuries. It has often been suggested that the development of more ornate music was the primary cause for this change. But other and perhaps more pervasive factors were also operative: the use of Latin rather than the vernacular; the popular understanding of the Mass either as a drama to be contemplated or as an occasion for receiving the graces of God; a spirituality concentrating on awe and wonder before the mysterious and majestic presence of the divine. A Christian merely had to be present in order to listen to a language understood by few, to see an action staged with great ceremony in a distant sanctuary, and to adore the sacred species consecrated during the eucharistic prayer. During the ninth and tenth centuries this prayer, once proclaimed aloud, came to be recited silently. Now excluded from the very center of the eucharistic liturgy, the people had even less motiviation to participate in the other parts of the celebration. The assembly became a congregation of mute spectators left to its private contemplation and meditation while clergy and choir enacted the divine drama.

Although the Churches of the Reformation promoted congregational singing, e.g. the Lutheran chorale in Germany and psalmody in Geneva, the restoration of the tradition of the assembly's musical participation does not seem to have been of major concern during the Catholic Counter-Reformation. The Council of Trent (1545-1563), while repudiating numerous doctrinal attacks on the Mass and correcting practical abuses, apparently gave no thought to restoring the proper part of the assembly in the liturgy. Perhaps the acrimonious polemic of the time militated against this. In a report sent in June 1543 to Pope Paul II, the bishop of Vienne in France attacked the Protestant German hymns which, in his words, "go contrary to the authority of the Supreme Pontiffs, the Mass, the good works, and the established customs of religious people on the one hand and praise their (i.e. the Reformers') new rites and dogmas on the other."[19] Yet not all were so adamantly opposed. St. Peter Canisius (1521-1597), for example, encouraged vernacular singing in German, probably in conjunction with the sermon.[20] And, as we shall see, various local attempts were undertaken in sixteenth and seventeenth century Germany to have the people sing vernacular hymns during Low Masses. Nevertheless, this singing accompanied the liturgy and was not integral to it.

The early nineteenth century heard a few scattered voices calling for liturgical reform. For example, J.B. Hirscher (1788-1865), one of the founders of the University of Tubingen, strongly advocated that the faithful participate during Mass and not merely assist at it. Among his proposals for reform were the elimination of hymn singing during Mass, the celebration of Mass in the vernacular, and communal singing of the Ordinary.[21] In spite of such calls for change, it was only during the second half of the century that the seeds for a theologically and historically sound renewal of the liturgy were sown, especially through the influence of the Benedictine monks in Germany, Belgium, and France.

The pontificate of Pius X (1903-1914) initiated a decisive period of liturgical renewal, particularly in regard to the quality of liturgical music and the participation of the people. The Pope's love of tradition, his experience as a parish priest, and his devotion to plainsong were all reflected in his motu proprio *Tra le sollicitudini* (1903), which unequivocally stated that the faithful were to take "an active part in the sacred mysteries and in the solemn public prayers of the Church" (Introduction). Pius emphasized that music is "an integral part of the liturgy" (n.1) and requested that Gregorian chant "be restored to the use of the people, so that they may take a more active part in the offices as they did in former times" (n.3).[22] Succeeding decades witnessed enthusiastic attempts to implement the Pope's desire for a restoration of the chant as the song of the people. Though somewhat successful in monasteries, seminaries, and religious houses, such efforts generally proved less fruitful in most parishes. Sung Vespers or Compline with the participation of the people attained a certain measure of popularity in some areas, but the music of the Mass usually remained under the domain of the choir alone. Meanwhile, others were striving to involve the people more fully in the celebration of the Low Mass, and it was this endeavor which, at least on a practical level, was more influential in restoring the sung participation of the assembly.

Since the end of the nineteenth century translations of the missal were permitted, allowing the people to follow in the vernacular the prayers of the priest. But in the 1920s and 1930s, under the influence of the growing liturgical movement in Germany, Belgium, and elsewhere, the desire for more communal participation gave birth to the dialogue Mass where the people responded in Latin to the priest. At times the faithful even recited the Latin texts of the Ordinary together with the priest or said these parts in the vernacular while the priest said them in Latin. This form of participation took place within the framework of the Low Mass and left its rubrics untouched. It was not long before the dialogue Mass incorporated certain elements of a long-standing German tradition, namely that of the *Singmesse.*

In 1592 the synod of Breslau allowed German hymns to be sung at Solemn and High Masses both as a replacement for the gradual and after communion. A few years later, in 1605, the Cantual of Mainz extended this permission to include vernacular hymnody at the offertory, after the Agnus Dei, and during communion. The same book allowed German hymns to be sung throughout the Low Mass except during the gospel, elevation, and final blessing. Undoubtedly the popularity of hymn singing in the Lutheran liturgy influenced the giving of this permission. By the eighteenth century, as a result of the growing recognition of this custom's pastoral advantages, German hymns could be substituted for all parts of the Ordinary at both High and Low Masses. This type of celebration, known as the *Singmesse,* allowed the Mass to be sung in smaller churches which lacked the vocal and instrumental resources necessary for the orchestral Masses popular at the time. And yet the *Singmesse* form was also expanded by certain composers who wrote settings for choir, congregation, and instruments. In spite of many attacks, the *Singmesse* met with great acceptance in certain areas of Germany, although it was only in 1943 that Rome officially recognized or at least "most kindly tolerated" the *Singmesse,* but for Germany alone.[23]

In the 1930's there developed a form of celebration known as the German *Betsingmesse* which combined elements from both the dialogue Mass and the *Singmesse,* i.e., the people responding in Latin to the priest and singing vernacular hymns to accord with various parts of the liturgy. Similar forms of participation soon became popular in other countries, such as France and the United States. The essential problem, however, was that the singing of the assembly in the vernacular merely paralleled the action of the priest. Other than those few instances when the whole assembly joined in singing plainsong during a High or Solemn Mass, the people were singing during the Mass and not as an integral part of it.

The desire for a more immediate participation in the liturgy was often expressed during the years immediately preceding the Second Vatican Council. Intensive study and discussion on the nature of the Church as well as on the liturgy as an action of God's people furthered the cause. Doubts were increasingly raised about the pastoral feasibility of plainsong as an effective form of sung participation in most parishes. There were also many requests that the vernacular be reintroduced, at least in some parts of the liturgy. Confronted with an increasing groundswell of support for liturgical reform, the Roman documents of the period reacted by reinforcing three general principles: 1) the inviolability of the Latin text; 2) the need for the assembly to sing at least the Ordinary of the Mass in the somewhat simple Gregorian melodies; 3) the distinction between the Sung Mass and the Low Mass. For example, Pope Pius XII's encyclical *Mediator Dei* (November 30, 1946) encouraged the use of Gregorian chant at Sung Masses and the celebration of Sunday Vespers. At Low Masses the people were either to "answer the priest in an orderly and fitting manner, or sing hymns suitable to the different parts of the Mass, or do both" (n.105).[24] In his letter on sacred music, i.e. *Musicae sacrae disciplina* (December 25, 1955), Pius somewhat reluctantly allowed popular vernacular hymns to be sung after the words of the liturgy were sung in Latin where the local bishop, in the face of an old and immemorial custom, believed he could not prudently forbid the practice. The same general directives were repeated by the September 3, 1958 *Instruction on Sacred Music and the Sacred Liturgy* issued by the Sacred Congregation of Rites.

The Magna Carta of the assembly's recovery of its rightful role within the liturgy is, of course, Vatican II's *Constitution on the Sacred Liturgy* (December 4, 1963). The document's most basic principle is that the Church's worship is an action of the community, but an action which is hierarchical. "Liturgical services pertain to the whole body of the Church; they manifest it and have effects upon it; but they concern the individual members of the Church in different ways, according to their differing rank, office, and actual participation" (n.26). It is this communal nature of the celebration which requires "the presence and active participation of the faithful" (n.27). And "to promote active participation, the people should be encouraged to take part by means of acclamations, responses, psalmody, antiphons, and song . . . ." (n.30).

Although the *Constitution* maintains that the "use of Latin is to be preserved in the Latin rite," the difficulty of praying in a foreign language is confronted: the vernacular "frequently may be of great advantage to the people . . . this will apply in the first place to the readings and directives, and to some of the prayers and chants . . ." (n.56). But since the whole Mass and in fact all liturgy "pertain to the people," permission to use the vernacular was broadened in the years subsequent to the Council to include all forms of liturgical celebration. The Fathers of the Council acknowledge "Gregorian chant as specially suited to the Roman liturgy" and "therefore, other things being equal, it should be given pride of place in liturgical services" (n.116). Yet the fundamental norm for the choice of music is to enable "the whole body of the faithful . . . to contribute that active participation which is rightly theirs" (n.114).

The guidelines for liturgical reform enunciated by the Council were scrupulously observed by the artisans of the revised rites which appeared in years to follow. All the rites presume the presence and participation of a community of people. All call for common song. The Order of Mass, making no distinction between the High Mass and the Low Mass, not only encourages the song of the assembly but even considers this normative. The sacramental and other rites incorporate psalmody, responses, and acclamations: they also leave room for the singing of hymns. The Liturgy of the Hours has been restored as the prayer of the whole Church and is considered to achieve its greatest beauty and prayerfulness when sung. The song of the people in the revised liturgy is not seen as an artistic exercise of devotion or as busywork: it is, rather, the restoration of an ancient tradition of a people expressing their unity of hearts and minds as they offer praise to the Father.

Documentation

Constitution on the Sacred Liturgy

14. Mother Church earnestly desires that all the faithful should be led to that full, conscious, and active participation in liturgical celebrations which is demanded by the very nature of the liturgy. Such participation by the Christian people as "a chosen race, a royal priesthood, a holy nation, a redeemed people" (1 Pet. 2:9; cf. 2:4-5) is their right and duty by reason of their baptism. In the restoration and promotion of the sacred liturgy, this full and active participation by all the people is the aim to be considered before all else; for it is the primary and indispensable source from which the faithful are to derive the true Christian spirit; and therefore pastors of souls must zealously strive to achieve it, by means of the necessary instruction, in all their pastoral work.

28. In liturgical celebrations each person, minister or layman, who has an office to perform, should do all of, but only, those parts which

pertain to his office by the nature of the rite and the principles of liturgy.

30. To promote active participation, the people should be encouraged to take part by means of acclamations, responses, psalmody, and songs, as well as by means of actions, gestures, and bodily attitudes. And at the proper times all should observe a reverent silence.

113. Liturgical worship is given a more noble form when the divine offices are celebrated solemnly in song, with the assistance of sacred ministers and the active participation of the people.

114. . . . . bishops and other pastors of souls must be at pains to ensure that, whenever the sacred action is to be celebrated with song, the whole body of the faithful may be able to contribute that active participation which is rightly theirs, as laid down in Art. 28 and 30.

18. Religious singing by the people is to be skillfully fostered, so that in devotions and sacred exercises, as also during liturgical services, the voices of the faithful may ring out according to the norms and requirements of the rubrics.

Instruction for the Proper Implementation of the Constitution on the Sacred Liturgy

59. Pastors of souls shall carefully see to it that the faithful, more particularly the members of lay religious associations, also know how to say or to sing together in the Latin language those parts of the Ordinary of the Mass which pertain to them, especially with the use of simpler melodies.

Instruction on Music in the Liturgy

15. The faithful fulfill their liturgical role by making that full, conscious and active participation which is demanded by the nature of the liturgy itself and which is, by reason of baptism, the right and duty of the Christian people. This participation
a) Should be above all internal, in the sense that by it the faithful join their minds to what they pronounce or hear, and cooperate with heavenly grace;
b) Must be, on the other hand, external also, that is, such as to show the internal participation by gesture and bodily attitudes, by the acclamations, responses, and singing.
The faithful should also be taught to unite themselves interiorly to what the ministers or choir sing, so that by listening to them they may raise their minds to God.

16. One cannot find anything more religious and more joyful in sacred celebrations than a whole congregation expressing its faith and devotion in song. Therefore the active participation of the whole people, which is shown in singing, is to be carefully promoted as follows:
a) It should first of all include acclamations, responses to the

greetings of the priest and ministers and to the prayers of litany form, and also antiphons and psalms, refrains or repeated responses, hymns and canticles.

b) Through suitable instruction and practices, the people should be gradually led to a fuller—indeed, to a complete—participation in those parts of the singing which pertain to them.

c) Some of the people's song, however, especially if the faithful have not yet been sufficiently instructed, or if musical settings for several voices are used, can be handed over to the choir alone, provided that the people are not excluded from those parts that concern them. But the usage of entrusting to the choir alone the entire singing of the whole Proper and of the whole Ordinary, to the complete exclusion of the people's participation in the singing, is to be deprecated.

17. At the proper times, all should observe a reverent silence. Through it the faithful are not only not considered as extraneous or dumb spectators at the liturgical service, but are associated more intimately in the mystery that is being celebrated, thanks to that interior disposition which derives from the word of God that they have heard, from the songs and prayers that have been uttered, and from spiritual union with the priest in the parts that he says or sings himself.

18. . . . The formation of the whole people in singing should be seriously and patiently undertaken together with liturgical instruction, according to the age, status and way of life of the faithful, and the degree of their religious culture; this should be done even from the first years of education in elementary schools.

General Instruction of the Roman Missal

19. The faithful who gather to await the Lord's coming are urged by the Apostle Paul to sing psalms, hymns, and spiritual canticles (see Col. 3:16). Song is the sign of the heart's joy (see Acts 2:46), and St. Augustine said: "To sing belongs to lovers." Even in antiquity it was proverbial to say: "He prays twice who sings well." Singing should be widely used at Mass, depending on the type of people and the capability of each congregation, but it is not always necessary to sing all the texts which were composed for singing. Preference should be given to more significant parts, especially those to be sung by priest or ministers with the people responding or to those to be sung by the priest and people together. Since people frequently come together from different countries, it is desirable that they know how to sing together at least some parts of the Ordinary of the Mass in Latin, especially the profession of faith and the Lord's Prayer, set to simple melodies.

58. Everyone in the eucharistic assembly has the right and duty to take his own part according to the diversity of orders and functions. Whether minister or layman, everyone should do that and only that which belongs to him, so that in the liturgy the Church may be seen as composed of various orders and ministries.

62. In the celebration of Mass the faithful are a holy people, a chosen race, a royal priesthood, giving thanks to the Father and offering the victim and themselves not only through the hands of the priest but also with him. They should make this clear by their deep sense of religion and their charity to everyone who shares in the celebration . . . . They should become one in hearing the word of God, joining in prayers and song, and in the common offering of sacrifice and sharing of the Lord's table.

Third Instruction on the Correct Implementation of the Constitution on the Sacred Liturgy

3c. All means must be used to promote singing by the people.

Music in Catholic Worship

34. Music for the congregation must be within its members' performance capability. The congregation must be comfortable and secure with what they are doing in order to celebrate well.

Liturgical Music Today

63. The entire worshiping assembly exercises a ministry of music. Some members of the community, however, are recognized for the special gifts they exhibit in leading the musical praise and thanksgiving of Christian assemblies. These are the pastoral musicians, whose ministry is especially cherished by the Church.

70. A community will not grow in its ability either to appreciate or express its role in musical liturgy if each celebration is thought of as a discrete moment. A long-range plan must be developed which identifies how music will be used in the parish and how new music will be learned. The abilities of the congregation should never be misjudged. Some cannot or will not sing, for whatever reason. Most will take part, and will enjoy learning new music if they have effective leaders.

Reflection

Christian worship is found neither in ritual books, nor in liturgical commentaries, nor in rubrical directives. To worship is to do something: it is an action of a people. Before there can be any worship there must be a people, an assembly of believers who have gathered together in response to the call of God. By their very presence and by the use of symbol, sign, and word these people, themselves being the primary symbol of worship, affirm and proclaim their shared faith and life in Christ Jesus. When the *Constitution on the Sacred Liturgy* speaks of the "full and active participation by all the people" in the liturgy (n.14), it touches on the very essence of worship, which is not stage drama performed by actors but rather affirmation, celebration, feast, and, above all, prayer. These are personal actions that admit no surrogates. They demand that all be active participants.

Human involvement in religious ritual has long known the use of music, especially singing. This is no less true of Christian worship. In the liturgy of the Church, common song is a means of establishing a bond among members, of insuring group integration, of expressing that unity of purpose rooted in the waters of baptism. When Christians sing together, they minister to one another: there is mutual support as each person lends a voice to the song of the community and thereby encourages others to do likewise. Through sung prayer the assembly proclaims that its members form an Easter people who as one body joyfully announce the good news of Christ. Singing is a sign that something important happens when these people come together. It is an unequalled confession of that praise which is the hallmark of a holy people. Yet common song, if it is to be authentic prayer, must be expressive of people truly engaged in communion with God and others. It must come from persons whose hands faithfully carry out the work of God, for unless the gospel message is lived outside the liturgy, it cannot be truly celebrated within it.

In some communities the goal of a singing assembly is, unfortunately, still to be attained. To reestablish the long lost tradition of a people who express their faith in song is a challenge requiring patience, constant effort, judicious selection of music and accompaniment, and ongoing encouragement. Yet the problem has another dimension. Common song flows naturally when values are commonly shared, when people have experienced something worth singing about. Witness, for example, the enthusiastic and contagious singing at Marriage Encounters, Cursillo meetings, and charismatic prayer gatherings. If values are strong, then the celebration of these values will be strong, and this will be reflected in the assembly's sung prayer.

The music of a prayerful people, though centered upon the common song of the whole assembly, embraces many rhythms and elicits many roles. There are moments when all participants join in acclamations, responses to greetings and litanies, psalmody (especially the antiphons), and hymns. Pastoral musicians are to lead and facilitate this common expression of faith. There are also moments when the voice of the presider or deacon alone is raised in song. Additionally, there are those moments when musicians nourish and sustain the prayer quality of the celebration through their own prayerful artistry. It is only when there is a balance of roles, of moments to listen, to reflect, and to respond, that the sung prayer of the whole assembly appears for what it truly is, namely the expression of a living, unified people in joyful dialogue with God and with one another.

Suggested Questions for Discussion

1. On what occasions of life do people most like to sing? Why?
2. What images are suggested by the phrase "the singing assembly"?

3. Why is the sung prayer of the assembly central to all ministries of music?
4. How can the members of the assembly be assisted to experience common song as prayer?
5. How can ministers of music most effectively facilitate and stimulate the song of the assembly?
6. What are some obstacles that might hinder people from singing? How can they be overcome?
7. What techniques can be employed to introduce new music to the assembly? Which are most successful? Why?
8. What are the criteria for judging whether music is within the performance capability of the members of the congregation (*Music in Catholic Worship* n.34)?

Bibliography

Batastini, Robert. "Catholics Can Sing." *Today's Parish* 11:6 (September 1979), pp.20-22.

Batastini, Robert. "Our People Just Don't Like to Sing? New Music: Step by Step." *Pastoral Music* 2:2 (December-January 1978), pp.46-47. Reprinted in *Pastoral Music in Practice*. Ed. by Virgil C. Funk and Gabe Huck. Washington, D.C.: National Association of Pastoral Musicians. Chicago: Liturgy Training Publications, 1981. pp.117-120.

Bauman, William. "Parish Song and the Struggle for Quality." *Liturgical Week Proceedings* 27 (1966), pp.182-185.

Cunningham, W. Patrick. "Free at Last! To Pray in Song." *Today's Parish* 12:6 (September 1980), pp.11-14.

Deiss, Lucien. *Persons in Liturgical Celebrations*. Trans. by Diane Karampas, ed. by Carol Kelly. Chicago: World Library Publications, 1978. pp.12-20.

Deiss, Lucien. *Spirit and Song of the New Liturgy*. Trans. by Lyla L. Haggard and Michael L. Mazzarese. Cincinnati: World Library of Sacred Music, 1970. pp. 28-36.

Foley, Edward. "The Congregation as Musician." *Pastoral Music* 2:4 (April-May 1978), pp. 32-35.

Funk, Virgil. "Making Music Work." *Today's Parish* 11:1 (January 1979), p.43.

Gelineau, Joseph. "Singing by the People." *Theology Digest* 9 (Autumn 1961), pp.155-159.

Gelineau, Joseph. *Voices and Instruments in Christian Worship: Principles, Laws, Applications*. Trans. by Clifford Howell. Collegeville: The Liturgical Press, 1964. pp.80-84.

Guentner, Francis J. "Congregational Singing." *New Catholic Encyclopedia* IV, pp.171-173.

Haller, Reginald B. "Congregational Singing." *New Catholic Encyclopedia* XVII, pp. 151-152.

Heywood, Robert B. "Let My People Sing." *Worship* 40:6 (June-July 1966), pp.349-360.

Huck, Gabe. "For the Assembly." *Touchstones for Liturgical Ministers.* Ed. by Virginia Sloyan. Washington, D.C.: The Liturgical Conference, 1978. pp.11-12.

Hume, Paul. "Yes, But Why Do We Have to Sing?" *Liturgical Week Proceedings* 26 (1965), pp.131-135.

Jungmann, Joseph. "Liturgy and Congregational Singing." *Pastoral Liturgy.* New York: Herder and Herder, 1962. pp.345-356.

Madden, Lawrence. "The Congregation's Active Participation in Performance." *Pastoral Music* 3:2 (December-January 1979), pp.10-11.

McNaspy, Clement J. "Helping Your Congregation to Participate." *Pastoral Music* 3:2 (December-January 1979), pp.31-34.

McNaspy, Clement J. "Yes, But Why Do We Have to Sing?" *Liturgical Week Proceedings* 26 (1965), pp.136-140.

Rivers, Clarence. "Yes, But Why Do We Have to Sing?" *Liturgical Week Proceedings* 26 (1965), pp.141-147.

St. Louis Jesuits. "The Congregation's Prayer." *Pastoral Music* 3:5 June-July 1979), pp.44-48.

Walsh, Edward. "Onward Christian Choristers." *Today's Parish* 11:4 (April 1979), pp.26-28.

Walsh, Eugene A. "Never on Sunday." *Today's Parish* 10:6 (September 1978), pp. 19-21.

2
Presider

2
Presider

Historical Background

In the early Christian community it was the bishop, the head of the local Church, who ordinarily presided over the weekly gathering of the people on the Lord's Day. With the clergy, i.e., the presbyters, deacons, and minor clerics, gathered about him, the bishop proclaimed in improvisational fashion the prayer of praise and thanksgiving over the bread and the wine. He often distributed the eucharist to those who were present. And as a formal liturgy of the word developed and became an ordinary part of the celebration of the eucharist, it was usually the bishop who preached, explaining to the faithful the scriptures that had just been read. With the addition of other structural elements to the liturgy, the bishop led various orations, extended the greeting at the beginning of the celebration, and did whatever was judged appropriate for the official leader of the community's prayer. He also presided at baptisms, ordinations of various ministers, vigils, morning and evening prayer, and other gatherings of the community. But as the number of Christians increased, it became more and more common for presbyters, in the bishop's absence, to lead the assembly in its prayer.

Lacking documentary evidence, we can only conjecture as to the musical role of the bishop or priest in the earliest centuries of Christian worship. Undoubtedly he joined the assembly in singing psalm responses, hymns, and other chants. There is reason to believe that by at least the sixth century the eucharistic prayer was proclaimed in a more formal song-speech style.[1] Years later, during the ninth and tenth centuries, this prayer came to be recited silently in the Roman rite, and yet its preface continued to be prayed aloud or sung in recitative fashion. The Our Father, serving since the late fourth century as a preparation for communion, may have been sung by the bishop or priest as early as the fifth century.[2] Other prayers traditionally sung by the presider are the orations or collects. Their recitative tones, always simple and restrained, were first notated in the Middle Ages and often differed according to locale and the type (e.g., monastic, cathedral) of church.

An informative source for the involvement of both presider and assisting clergy in the musical dynamic of the eucharist is Roman Ordo I, which depicts the celebration of the papal Mass toward the end of the seventh century.[3] Of special interest is the close connection between the pope and the members of the schola. It was the pontiff who, by signaling the schola when to conclude, governed the length of the psalmody which accompanied the entrance procession, the gathering and presentation of the gifts, and the communion procession. The same was true for the litanic Kyries. The pope intoned the Gloria and perhaps the Sanctus as well since this was the practice in Rome in the year 530.[4] Although the Ordo says nothing about the pope singing the orations, eucharistic prayer, and greetings, it testifies to his active role in the musical flow of the celebration. Ordo I also relates that the assisting subdeacons chanted the Sanctus, once a song of the assembly at large. Centuries to follow would see an acceleration of this practice whereby the assisting clergy usurped the chants of the people.

There was also another development, one pertaining to the role of the presider, which would strain the musical texture of the celebration and somewhat distend its structure. For centuries the ritual elements of the Mass, depending on their nature, were carried out either by the assembly at large or by individual ministers. At times all acted together as, for instance, when the whole body of the faithful raised its common voice in singing the Gloria. More often there was harmonious dialogue between minister and the other members of the assembly. Each person, acting either together with others or individually, had a distinct part. In time this distribution of roles was even reflected in the various liturgical books which appeared. The prayers of the presider were collected and gradually codified in books called sacramentaries; the readings were systematically gathered in various types of lectionaries; the texts and, eventually, melodies for the schola were placed in antiphonaries; the parts for the cantor were brought together in cantatoria. The constantly recurring chants of the people, however, did not require written form since their simple texts and melodies were known by heart. Separate books for presider, reader, cantor, and schola were required at liturgies celebrated with great ceremonial in cathedrals and major churches which had a full contingent of ministers and singers. This full ritual form was the forerunner of the former Solemn High Mass. In addition to this solemn form there was also the celebration of the Mass in smaller, often rural, churches which had no trained singers and lacked a variety of assisting ministers. Although documentary evidence is lacking, scholars have attempted to reconstruct this type of celebration.[5] The chants of the schola were simply omitted; the priest was probably assisted by a cleric who proclaimed the scriptures, helped prepare the gifts, and assumed the role of the psalmist; the people responded by singing the parts traditionally assigned to them. Eventually this form led to the High or Sung Mass.

There was still a third way of celebrating the eucharist. Known from at least the sixth century, it was encouraged by the growing practice of ordaining monks as priests.[6] For reasons of personal piety these priest-monks celebrated Mass daily and often alone. This private form received additional incentive during the early Middle Ages when the faithful began to give offerings or stipends with the request that Masses be celebrated for particular intentions. As this practice spread, numerous altars came to replace the customary one altar in monastic and other churches. At each altar stood a priest who celebrated Mass. He was unassisted, except on rare occasions by a cleric or server; there was no singing; all was said and done in soft whispers; everything took place at the altar itself; the priest assumed all the roles of the celebration, at times even responding to his own greetings. From this private celebration derived the Low Mass. Accompanying this phenomenon was the gradual incorporation of the chants and readings into the priest's book. Formerly several books, each designed for particular ministers, were normatively required for the celebration of the eucharist; now one book sufficed, and this would give rise to the missal. Texts meant to be sung were now recited. Elements pertaining to the assembly and its various ministers now were the property of the priest. In short, a diversity of roles and parts coalesced in the person of the priest whose quiet recitation of all texts further contributed to a ritual leveling.

This process of liturgical disintegration continued in the twelfth and thirteenth centuries. Since all the texts were now considered as belonging to the priest, he was required to say them even at Sung Masses. Thus the same set of texts was simultaneously being recited by the priest and sung by the choir. The singing served as a musical overlay to the quietly recited prayers of the presider. The fabric of the celebration disintegrated even further in regard to the eucharistic prayer. As the Sanctus was given elaborate polyphonic settings, the priest merely continued the canon while the choir sang the prolonged musical background. Eventually it became custom and then law that the Benedictus was sung after the consecration.[7]

The recent revision of the liturgical rites has restored the role of the presider as a true leader of the assembly's prayer. His ministry, always of fundamental importance, assumes fullest expression among a diversity of liturgical roles as he does "that and only that which belongs to him, so that in the liturgy the Church may be seen in its variety of orders and ministries" (*General Instruction of the Roman Missal* n.58). In accord with this principle, he does not expropriate ministries which are rightfully those of the people, deacon, reader, cantor, and choir. Nor does he by silent recitation duplicate the sung prayer of the community. Musically he serves the people by his own ministerial chants and, unless engaged in such actions as preparing the gifts or preparing the eucharistic bread and wine for their distribution, by lending his own voice to the sung prayer of the assembly.

Documentation

Instruction on Music in the Liturgy

8. For a liturgical service which is to be celebrated in sung form, whenever one can make a choice between various people, it is desirable that those who are known to be more proficient in singing be given preference. This is especially the case in more solemn liturgical celebrations and in those which either require more difficult singing, or are transmitted by radio or television. If, however, a choice of this kind cannot be made, and the priest or minister does not possess a voice for the proper execution of the singing, he can render without singing one or more of the more difficult parts which pertain to him, reciting them in a loud and distinct voice. However, this must not be done merely for the convenience of the priest or minister.

14. The priest, acting in the person of Christ, presides over the gathered assembly. Since the prayers which are said or sung by him aloud are proclaimed in the name of the entire holy people and of all present, they should be devoutly listened to by all.

26. The priest, the sacred ministers . . . . should perform the parts assigned to them in a way which is comprehensible to the people, in order that the responses of the people, when the rite requires it, may be made easy and spontaneous. It is desirable that the priest, and the ministers of every degree, should join their voices to the voice of the whole faithful in those parts which concern the people.

General Instruction of the Roman Missal

60. A presbyter as celebrant also presides over the assembly in the person of Christ, leads it in prayer, proclaims the message of salvation, leads the people in offering sacrifice through Christ in the Spirit to the Father, and shares with them the bread of eternal life. At the eucharist he should serve God and the people with dignity and humility. By his actions and by his proclamation of the word he should impress upon the faithful the living presence of Christ.

Music in Catholic Worship

21. No other single factor affects the liturgy as much as the attitude, style, and bearing of the celebrant: his sincere faith and warmth as he welcomes the worshipping community; his human naturalness combined with dignity and seriousness as he breaks the Break of Word and Eucharist.

22. The style and pattern of song ought to increase the effectiveness of a good celebrant. His role is enhanced when he is capable of rendering some of his parts in song, and he should be encouraged to do so. What he cannot sing well and effectively he ought to recite. If capable of singing, he ought, for the sake of the people, to rehearse carefully the sung parts that contribute to their celebration.

Liturgical Music Today

66. Clergy and musicians should strive for mutual respect and cooperation in the achievement of their common goals.

67. As the assembly's principal leaders, priests and deacons must continue to be mindful of their own musical role in the liturgy. Priests should grow more familiar with chanting the presidential prayers of the Mass and other rites.

Reflection

Before all else the presider at worship is a member of the assembly. He serves within it. He is the prayer leader of a people who, at God's invitation, gather to listen, respond, offer praise and thanksgiving, and share the food of eternal life. Just as music is normative to the liturgical prayer of this people, so music is integral to the ministry of those who preside within this community. If the assembly is to be a singing assembly, then its presider must be a singing presider who joins the assembly in its common song. Failure to do so creates a vacuum within the chorus of hearts and minds uplifted in praise of the Father. The bishop or priest who sings with the people sets the tone for their song. When he sings with enthusiasm and joy, others will certainly follow. His participation is a sign that common song is not an addition to the liturgy but is integral to an action which by its very nature is the joyful and shared proclamation of the good news of Christ.

The presider not only is to join the common song of the assembly but is also called upon to sing certain ministerial chants. In the days of the High Mass these were prescribed by the rubrics. Today there is much freedom: there are many options. Yet selecting which presidential chants to sing is not a matter of personal whim or fancy since the nature of the celebration and the relative importance of its structural elements are determinative. The vocal abilities of individual presiders also need be considered. Among the primary chants of the presider would be the dialogue opening the eucharistic prayer, the preface expressing the motive for eucharistic praise, and the doxology which sums up the whole consecratory prayer. The lyrical quality and ritual importance of these parts call for more than a simple recitation. Other consecratory prayers, such as the blessing of the baptismal water and the blessing of the oil of the sick, also elicit sung proclamation. On occasions certain orations, such as the Opening Prayer and the Prayer after Communion, may also lend themselves to sung prayer. Yet it is not easy for many priests to sing these chants. In the past choral music was fostered in seminaries: instruction and practice in liturgical music were part of the seminary curriculum. Unfortunately, this is not always the case today. Furthermore, the transition from Latin to English often poses a psychological barrier to priests trained in the Latin chants. As a result many presiders are not comfortable singing alone. They need and often desire encouragement, support, and perhaps some practical help from the pastoral musician. And there is, of course, no substitute for practicing beforehand.

The musical ministry of the presider also extends to the various musicians in the community. It is axiomatic that liturgical ministries either support one another or weaken one another. They do not exist in isolation since they flow from a communality of service rooted in the baptismal nature of the Church. As for his part, the priest must respect the roles and talents of all who minister within the assembly. As presider and orchestrator of the whole celebration, he must be sensitive to its rhythms of sung prayer, spoken prayer, silent prayer. Though not an expert on musical technique, he can help musicians appreciate and evaluate the prayer quality of their particular ministry. Are they actually serving this particular assembly? Is their musical art expressive of prayer? Does it elicit prayer from this particular people? Through gentle leadership the priest can assist all pastoral musicians to grow in their role of service. He can encourage their further education, especially in the art of musical liturgy. His own openness and willingness to dialogue set an example for others to follow. He can facilitate communication between musicians and other ministers and also among those who share the musical ministry in the community. At planning sessions he participates not as a domineering autocrat but as a minister whose insights reflect the living tradition of the Church and the experience of the whole local community.

The *General Instruction of the Roman Missal* says that the presider "by his actions . . . . should impress upon the faithful the living presence of Christ" (n.61). This presence of the Lord is experienced in a unique way when the prayer of the assembly is sung prayer. The quality of this prayer depends ever so much on the leadership role of the presider. His participation, enthusiasm, and support often mark the difference between the "singing of a congregation" and the sung prayer of a joyous people expressing their unity in the Christ present and alive among his members.

Suggested Questions for Discussion

1. What impact does the singing or nonsinging of the presider have on the singing of the assembly?
2. How can presiders be made aware of the importance of their musical role?
3. What factors would determine the ministerial chants to be sung by the presider at a particular celebration?
4. In what practical ways can pastoral musicians assist presiders to sing?
5. Do the musical settings found in the Sacramentary help or hinder the singing of the presider's ministerial chants?
6. In what practical ways can the parish priest encourage the growth of the community's pastoral musicians?
7. To what extent should the presider be involved in planning the liturgy? In planning the music?

Bibliography

Deiss, Lucien. *Persons in Liturgical Celebrations*, pp. 54-56.

Deiss, Lucien. *Spirit and Song of the New Liturgy*, pp.22-27.

Faulkner, Quentin. "Teaching Music to Future Priests." *Liturgy* 24:6 (November-December 1979), pp.34-39.

Gelineau, Joseph. *Voices and Instruments in Christian Worship*, pp.73-75.

Gohm, Bert. "Do You, Father, Help the Musician?" *Pastoral Music* 5:3 (February-March 1981), pp.14-15.

Hovda, Robert W. "For Presiders/Preachers." *Touchstones for Liturgical Ministers.* Ed. by Virginia Sloyan. pp.27-28.

Jabusch, Willard F. "Priestly Ministry of Music." *Chicago Studies* 14:1 (Spring 1975), pp.37-47.

Kelly, Columba. "The Best Celebrant Sings It." *Pastoral Music* 2:4 (April-May 1978), pp.30-31.

McKenna, Edward. "We Don't Always Follow His Sermons But His Singing Is Contagious." *Pastoral Music* 4:1 (October-November 1979), pp.8-10.

Smith, Gregory. "Be Your Own Judge." *Pastoral Music* 2:2 (December-January 1978), pp.12-16.

Smith, Gregory. "Rich Dividends for the Priest Who Plans." *Pastoral Music* 2:6 (August-September 1978), pp.12-14.

Winterlin, John. "Father, Pay Attention to Music." *Pastoral Music* 3:4 (April-May 1979), pp.14-15.

Zsigray, Joseph. "Give Respect and Understanding." *Pastoral Music* 3:2 (December-January 1979), pp.12-14.

3

Deacon

3
Deacon

Historical Background

Although service, i.e., *diakonia* in Greek, was a hallmark of all who formed the early Christian community, certain of its members were charged with a special role of service. The classical scriptural text associated with the origin of these ministers, designated as deacons, is Acts 6:1-6 where seven men "of good reputation, full of the spirit and of wisdom" were selected to serve the needs of the Greek-speaking widows in Jerusalem. Eventually the diaconal role was formally structured, although the precise nature of this ministry varied from place to place. Deacons were considered as assistants to the bishop, as being the "eye of the Church" or as "servants of the Church" in carrying out various charitable tasks within the community, especially the care of the poor. They also preached the word of God and instructed the faithful. Inasmuch as there is a close relationship between service of neighbor and worship of God, deacons quite naturally assumed a prominent role when the community gathered for common prayer.

The liturgical role of the deacon was generally one of promoting good order within the assembly and acting as a link between the presider and the people by facilitating the dynamics of the celebration. Deacons led litanies, provided directions for standing and kneeling, prepared the altar and the gifts for the eucharist, assisted the presider at the altar, helped break the eucharistic bread, distributed communion especially as ministers of the cup, and gave various dismissals, e.g., the dismissal of the catechumens at the conclusion of the liturgy of the word and that of the whole assembly at the end of Mass. They also played a prominent role in the celebration of baptism, in the reconciliation of penitents, and in various prayer services. In the East deacons also served as ushers, standing at the door of the church and forbidding entrance to latecomers and nonbelievers.

By the end of the fourth century some deacons served as singers of the psalms. St. Athanasius (c.296-373), for example, called upon the people in Alexandria to respond after each verse of a psalm "sung by a deacon."[1] A short time later Egeria, in the account of her travels to the East, reports that the deacon sang one of the psalms at the office in Jerusalem.[2] In succeeding centuries, if we are to believe certain burial inscriptions, a number of deacons attained great renown as psalmists.[3] It was even customary at Rome to ordain deacons by reason of their vocal talent. To eliminate this abuse Pope Gregory I (590-604) in 595 decreed that deacons, called to the office of preaching and almsgiving, "during the solemnization of Masses are not to sing and may perform the office of reading only the gospel . . . . The psalms and the other readings should be done by subdeacons or, if necessity requires it, by those in minor orders."[4] This prohibition notwithstanding, later documents show that deacons continued to function as cantors.[5]

In some regions the deacon was responsible for organizing the whole liturgy of the word. A fifth century council of Toledo stated that the deacon is to "distribute and hear (sung) the lessons and responses in the metropolitan city, so that no one reads or sings the gospel, epistle or any reading whatever without it having been arranged beforehand."[6] Still it was primarily the gospel which was entrusted to the deacon since, as a servant of Christ, he was considered a special exemplar of the Lord who was proclaimed in this text. Already at an early period a sung stylization of the readings, especially that of the gospel, seems to have been common. St. Augustine (354-430) speaks of a "solemn reading" (*solemniter legere*) of the Passion on Good Friday.[7] Since the text was of primary importance in proclaiming the word of God, no extensive musical expansion evolved. The pericope was proclaimed in a simple type of speech-song with appointed cadences and melodic inflections at certain points of punctuation. The purpose of such a plain recitative was to insure that the reading be heard by all in the assembly. Various forms of these lesson tones, with that for the gospel being somewhat more developed, were notated in the early Middle Ages.

In addition to proclaiming the gospel, the deacon also played a major role in the petitionary prayer which concluded the liturgy of the word. This prayer, known as early as the middle of the second century[8] and perhaps inherited from the synagogue service,[9] began with the presider inviting all to pray for a particular intention; the assembly then prayed in silence; finally the presider gathered up the unspoken petitions of all in a prayer addressed to the Father. In penitential seasons the assembly knelt during the periods of silence, and it was the deacon who directed the movement of the people with "Let us kneel" and "Arise." This tripartite schema was repeated as all prayed for various members of the universal and local community. It seems that Pope Gelasius (492-496) replaced this older form, which continued to survive in the Good Friday liturgy, with a model which originated in the East. Most probably it was the same Pope who transferred its position toward the beginning of the Mass.[10] In this new structure the deacon briefly announced a series of short intentions, and after each intention the assembly responded with the acclamation Kyrie eleison. Soon the Christe eleison was also employed. A further modification took place during the pontificate of Gregory the Great (590-604). Desirous of shortening the length of the liturgy, he drastically curtailed the litany so that only its acclamations remained. Although there is no direct evidence that, before the time of Gregory, the deacon and the assembly sang their parts, this is at least highly probable since the litanic form of the prayer with its constant repetition almost demands musical expression as has been the tradition in various eastern rites. It was only with the reforms initiated by Vatican II that this petitionary prayer, now known as the General Intercessions, was restored to the Roman Mass.

In the East, especially in the Coptic and Ethiopian rites, the role of the deacon as the one who gives directions and serves as the presider's link with the assembly is especially evident in various forms of the eucharistic prayer utilized in these liturgies. Throughout the course of the prayer, which is often punctuated by various acclamations and words of affirmation sung by the assembly, the deacon sings instructions to both the assisting priests, e.g., "Lift up your hands," and to the people, e.g., "Adore God with fear." Though such diaconal interventions did not enter the tradition of the eucharistic prayer in the West, an analogous practice is currently found in the Roman Church's eucharistic prayers when after the institution narrative a minister says or sings "Let us proclaim the mystery of faith" to elicit the assembly's acclamation expressing belief in the all-embracing mystery of Christ present in the celebration. Although the rubrics do not specify, recent custom has entrusted this invitation to the deacon. It is a practice which well accords with the history of the deacon's liturgical role.

Another longstanding diaconal chant, one which is often more ornate than that of the gospel, is the dismissal. Already in the fourth century the deacon concluded liturgical services by giving formal leave for the assembly to depart.[11] In the papal Mass of the late seventh century the pope signaled the deacon to give the dismissal, thus demonstrating the close connection between deacon and presider. The very nature of the dismissal as a cry led to the deacon pronouncing vigorously and then actually chanting the formula. Extensive melodies for the Roman Ite, missa est and its Gallican counterpart, the Benedicamus Domino, already existed by the tenth century.[12] The Roman formula was further enhanced by the practice of troping, i.e., singing individual syllables of an interpolated text to the notes of the chant's melissma.

Two of the most traditional diaconal chants occur within the Paschal Vigil when the deacon, while carrying the lighted Easter Candle into the darkened church, chants the threefold "Light of Christ" and then, after arriving in the sanctuary, sings the *Praeconium Paschale* or *Exsultet*. The origin of this ceremony is most probably found in the ancient *Lucenarium* which evolved from the custom of lighting lamps in the house every evening. In time this family observance became the nucleus for a community service, i.e., the *Lucenarium*, with psalms, hymns, and prayers. Since it was the deacon who brought in the candle at this prayer service, it was natural that he would carry in the Easter Candle at the Vigil and sing the chants associated with it. Although a special Easter Candle ceremony was long in use elsewhere, it entered the papal liturgy only in the twelfth century as a transplant from Frankish lands. Initially the hymn in honor of the candle was improvised by the deacon, and eventually written down. Several examples of such texts have survived in their entirety. The *Exsultet*, so named from its opening Latin word, has been attributed to St. Ambrose (c.339-397), but it is more probably the creation of an anonymous monk or cleric at work in northern Italy or in Gaul during the seventh century. Its text draws upon the thought of Ambrose, Augustine, and other writers in poetically proclaiming the meaning of the Paschal event. During the Middle Ages in southern Italy the text of the hymn with musical notation was written on long scrolls. Illuminated pictures, illustrating the text, were painted upside down on the scroll so that the assembly could see depicted what was being sung as the deacon progressively unfolded the parchment over the front of the ambo.

The longstanding musical role of the deacon continues today, although it has been somewhat modified. In the former Solemn High Mass the deacon always chanted the gospel. Although the second edition of the Introduction to the Lectionary says that the readings "may be sung in a way suitable to different languages" (n.14), in practice they are most often proclaimed without chanted recitative. This preserves the rhythm of alternating spoken text with sung text in the celebration of the word. Furthermore, some question whether a melodic proclamation accords with the literary genre of most scriptural pericopes and effectively enhances their meaning. On the other hand, the restoration of the General Intercessions in the Roman Mass allows the deacon to exercise one of his most ancient roles, namely that of announcing the various intentions within the litanic prayer. When singing contributes to their prayerful quality, these intentions are preferably sung. They may be sung by the deacon, a cantor, or another person. When the deacon does so, he is faithful to a tradition which extends back to the formative years of the liturgy itself. The deacon, by custom, invites the assembly to proclaim the mystery of faith during the eucharistic prayer; he also dismisses the people at the conclusion of the liturgy. In both instances chant is appropriate.

In other liturgical services the musical function of the deacon has either been viewed more realistically or been extended. The *Exsultet* of the Easter Vigil is retained as a diaconal chant and yet, if necessary, it may be sung by one who is not a deacon. And since the deacon may now preside at certain liturgical celebrations, he may sing those texts traditionally reserved to the presidential role, e.g., invitations, greetings, orations, and other prayers.

Documentation

General Instruction of the Roman Missal

61. The deacon, whose order was held in high honor in the early Church, has first place upon the ministers. He proclaims the gospel, preaches, leads the general intercessions of the faithful, assists the priest, gives communion to the faithful, in particular ministering the chalice, and gives direction to the congregation.

71. If there are several persons present who can exercise the same ministry, different parts of it may be assigned to them. For example, one deacon may take the sung parts, another serve at the altar.

Liturgical Music Today

67. As the assembly's principal liturgical leaders, priests and deacons must continue to be mindful of their own musical role in the liturgy . . . . Deacons . . . in the admonitions, exhortations, and especially in the litanies of the third penitential rite and in the general intercessions of the Mass, have a significant role to play in worship.

Reflection

The deacon is ordained to serve the community as a minister of charity, word, and altar. His liturgical role, always to mirror his general service to the community, is varied. He may function as the presider at baptism, the liturgy of the hours, exposition and benediction of the Blessed Sacrament, and liturgies of the word. When delegated, the deacon may witness Christian marriage. He also proclaims the gospel and may preach the homily. But his primary liturgical ministry at the eucharistic celebration as well as on certain other occasions is to assist the bishop or the priest. Here the deacon acts as an enabler and, as such, facilitates the flow of the liturgy with its rhythm of actions, words, and music.

In the Byzantine tradition the deacon is considered as an "angel of prayer." Like the angels in Jacob's vision who ascended and descended the ladder rising to heaven, the deacon comes and goes as a "messenger" between the presider and the people. He has also been compared to the Holy Spirit for he energizes the prayer of the assembly. In the Roman rite of diaconal ordination the bishop prays that the deacon may "excel in unassuming authority, in self-discipline." These traits, characteristic of the entire diaconal ministry and indeed of all ministry, most aptly describe the musical role of the deacon as he assists the presider. The deacon's ministerial chants are few and usually modest. His role is not one of virtuoso singing, but one of sincere, direct, and honest heralding. To do this well requires a reverence for ritual and for musical ritual in particular. It entails an entering into the spirit of sung prayer. It necessitates a sensitivity to particular assemblies and to particular occasions in selecting which texts to sing. In his own way the deacon contributes in no small measure to the musical prayer of the assembly of which he is both servant and member.

Suggested Questions for Discussion

1. What factors would determine the diaconal chants to be sung at a particular celebration?
2. What is the effect on a celebration when the deacon's chants are sung but those of the presider are recited? Or when those of the presider are sung and those of the deacon are recited?
3. In what practical ways can pastoral musicians assist deacons to sing?
4. Should the deacon work with the parish worship committee in planning those celebrations in which he ministers as deacon?

Bibliography

Deiss, Lucien. *Persons in Liturgical Celebrations*, pp.49-50.
Gelineau, Joseph. *Voices and Instruments in Christian Worship*, pp.75-77.
Hovda, Robert. "For Deacons." *Touchstones for Liturgical Ministers.* Ed. by Virgina Sloyan. pp.29-30.

4
Cantor

4

Cantor

Historical Background

The earliest counterpart to the Christian cantor may be found in the Jewish *Sheliach Tzibbur* who served as a volunteer leader of prayer in the synogogue.[1] Delegated by the community to speak on its behalf, the *Sheliach Tzibbur*, i.e., the "messenger of the people," led various prayers and proclaimed the word of God. Initially anyone could be called upon to assume this role of leadership. But eventually emphasis was placed upon this person possessing certain personal qualities and technical skills. Among the latter was musical expertise. In time there emerged the professional singer who was distinguished more for musical ability than for prayer leadership. An analogous evolution may well have occurred within the early development of Christian worship.

In both early Christianity as well as in Judaism there was apparently little if any differentiation between spoken prayer and sung prayer. An element of lyricism was endemic to all common prayer. Even the scripture readings seem to have been declaimed in a simple form of recitative. Since many members of the early Church were Jewish and were well acquainted with synagogal practices, it would have been natural that a volunteer, akin to the *Sheliach Tzibbur*, proclaimed the readings and led the psalmody in cantillated fashion. The early sources often designate this person as the reader, although there is also evidence of others fulfilling this role.[2]

Once the Church attained legal status following the Peace of Constantine in 313, it was given the opportunity to expand its ritual forms.

There is also reason to believe that the same was true of its music.[3] More technique was required. There was also a crystallization and elaboration of liturgical roles. It was precisely during this period that an institutionalization of the role of the singer appeared. A distinct office of a specially designated singer emerged. The *Canons of Laodicea*, a fourth century canonical document which may in fact summarize earlier legislation from the same century, decrees that "no one shall sing in the assembly except the canonical singers who mount the ambo and sing from the parchment."[4] The same collection mentions singers among those persons forbidden to visit inns.[5] It also enjoins readers and singers from wearing the stole.[6] This prohibition, undoubtedly occasioned by the desire of certain singers to attain ecclesiastical status rather than to minister as leaders of sung prayer, was reflected by St. Jerome (c.345-420) who cautioned that singers as well as readers and acolytes were to be more concerned with their morals than with their apparel.[7] A further witness for the new office of the singer is the *Apostolic Constitutions*. This treatise, probably written in Syria about 380, places "psalmists" among the lower clergy where they are usually ranked after the readers.[8]

In the western Church the evolution of the cantor was far from uniform. The primitive tradition of the reader-singer continued at least till the sixth century when St. Gregory of Tours (c.540-594) spoke of readers who were also charged with the chants.[9] It appears that schools of young readers were organized in some areas.[10] These youths, perhaps destined for the priesthood, were trained in both reading and singing skills. Such an institution may well have been the predecessor or model of the Roman schola cantorum. It is probable that in some areas soloists were permanently designated for this role; in others, any person endowed with a beautiful voice and requisite skill would, at the request of the deacon, exercise this ministry. It was done even by the deacon himself, although this practice was condemned at Rome by Pope Gregory I (590-604). Although the ministry of the cantor never became one of the official orders in the western Church, the role was closely associated with that of the clerical ministers. The *Statuta Ecclesiae Antiqua*, a canonical collection probably drawn up in fifth century Gaul, contains a blessing of the psalmist. The text reads: "The psalmist, i.e., the cantor, can assume his office of singing, without the knowledge of the bishop, by the command of the priest who says, 'Take care that you believe in your heart what you sing and that you practice what you believe'."[11]

The most celebrated group of cantors is the Roman schola cantorum whose establishment may well date to the pontificate of Pope Gregory I (590-604). Its role in the papal Mass at the end of the seventh century is described by Ordo I, which makes special mention of two soloists.[12] After the first reading a singer mounted one of the lower steps (*gradus*) of the ambo and from his book, i.e., the *cantatorium*, sang the response to the reading. Although the Ordo does not specify, this soloist was undoubtedly one of the subdeacons belonging to the schola. It is evident that no small importance was attached to this role since the names of the singers had to be announced to the pope before the liturgy and, once announced, no changes were permitted. After the psalm another soloist sang the Alleluia or, in certain penitential seasons, the Tract. Ordo I does not mention the assembly responding to the verses of the Gradual or repeating the Alleluia after the cantor: perhaps by this time the members of the schola had appropriated these parts, at least in the papal liturgy.

As choir schools, often patterned on the Roman model, were established in monastic and major churches, the pedagogical role of the cantor increased. An allusion to his function as a teacher is already found in the early seventh century when St. Isidore of Seville (c. 560-636) wrote that "the psalmist is in charge of the singing . . . and that which pertains to the technique of the chant."[13] Roman cantors, especially those entrusted with the musical instruction of the schola, traveled throughout Europe to establish schools of chant. As the music became more complex, they also served as directors of the singing. According to an eleventh century account, the cantor, holding a pastoral staff in his left hand as a sign of his dignity, directed the singers with his right hand in a type of chironomy. He also gave the pitch for the melody by singing an ascending and descending scale of five notes according to the particular mode of the composition.[14]

The role of the cantor as a solo singer, however, began to wane starting from the ninth and tenth centuries. He was gradually replaced by a select group of singers, often boy members of the schola, as the solo chants came to be sung by the whole body. Consequently, parts formerly found in the cantor's *cantatorium* were simply incorporated into the schola's antiphonary. The growth of polyphonic music, which required not one singer but a small ensemble of performers, also contributed to the decline of the cantor as a soloist. As part of this evolution the rank of the cantor or precentor in cathedral churches became an honorary position. A member of the cathedral chapter, usually ranked after the dean, received a honorarium for this task even though the musical functions were frequently carried out by others, often called succentors, trained in a musical art whose demands were becoming more extensive. In medieval England the precentor was assigned the first stall on the north side of the choir, and thus this side became known as the *cantoris* as contrasted with the *decani* or deacon's side on the south.

During the Baroque period the title of cantor was applied to the music director in the Lutheran Church. He was required to supervise the musical program in the parish, instruct the choristers, compose music when necessary, cooperate with the clergy in liturgical matters, and lead an exemplary life. The most famous of such cantors is Johann Sebastian Bach (1685-1750) who fulfilled this role at St. Thomas in Leipzig. In the Roman Church the role of the cantor, at least for all practical purposes, fell into disuse other than in certain religious congregations where three or four members of the community were appointed to intone the chant, serve as teachers of music, read the lessons of the office, take charge of the liturgical books, and perform such sundry tasks as caring for the lights in the choir and sweeping the refectory.[15]

The reforms mandated by Vatican II have restored the cantorial role to the Roman liturgy. Since common song is now a normative form of participation in all types of celebration, a leader is often required to encourage and lead this song. Even more important, the incorporation of a liturgy of the word in all the revised rites calls for the assembly to respond to the first reading by means of psalmody. By their very nature as lyrical compositions, the psalms are meant to be sung. This is most easily accomplished through responsorial singing where one person, i.e., the psalmist, sings the verses and all respond by means of a sung antiphon. The cantor acting as psalmist and general leader of the community's sung prayer continues one of the ancient and most venerable traditions of the Roman liturgy.

Documentation

Instruction on Music in the Liturgy

21. Provision should be made for at least one or two properly trained singers, especially where there is no possibility of setting up even a small choir. The singer will present some simpler musical settings, with the people taking part, and can lead and support the faithful as far as is needed. The presence of such a singer is desirable even in churches which have a choir, for those celebrations in which the choir cannot take part but which may fittingly be performed with some solemnity and therefore with singing.

General Instruction of the Roman Missal

64. There should be a cantor or a choirmaster to direct and encourage the people in singing. If there is no choir, the cantor leads the various songs, and the people take their own part.

67. The chanter of the psalms is to sing the psalm or other biblical song between the readings. He should be trained in the art of singing psalms and be able to speak clearly and distinctly.

Music in Catholic Worship

35. While there is no place in the liturgy for display of virtuosity for its own sake, artistry is valued, and an individual singer can effectively lead the assembly, attractively proclaim the Word of God in the psalm sung between the readings, and take his or her part in other responsorial singing. "Provision should be made for at least one or two properly trained singers, especially where there is no possibility of

setting up even a simple choir. The singer will present some simpler musical settings, with the people taking part, and can lead and support the faithful as far as is needed. The presence of such a singer is desirable, even in churches which have a choir, for those celebrations in which the choir cannot take part but which may fittingly be performed with some solemnity and therefore with singing." Although a cantor "cannot enhance the service of worship in the same way as a choir, a trained and competent cantor can perform an important ministry by leading the congregation in common sacred song and in responsorial singing."

Liturgical Music Today

68. Among music ministers, the cantor has come to be recognized as having a crucial role in the development of congregational singing. Besides being qualified to lead singing, he or she must have the skills to introduce and teach new music, and to encourage the assembly. This must be done with sensitivity so that the cantor does not intrude on the communal prayer or become manipulative. Introductions and announcements should be brief and avoid a homiletic style.

69. The cantor's role is distinct from that of the psalmist, whose ministry is the singing of the verses of the responsorial psalm and communion psalm. Frequently the two roles will be combined in one person.

Reflection

The ministry of the cantor, unlike that of the presider who leads the assembly in the totality of its prayer, is a specialized ministry since the cantor serves the community at particular moments of the celebration. It is a ministry which serves the people as they pray in song. Above all else the cantor is a minister of prayer, especially when singing the psalms but at other times as well.

Although musical and liturgical competence is indispensable, the cantorial ministry is not one of virtuosity or musical showmanship. It is to be a servant, acting on behalf of the assembly and on behalf of the prayer being sung. To elicit prayer or, more exactly, to create conditions that allow prayer to happen, the cantor enters into a relationship with a people. If the cantor is warm, gracious, and inviting, then the assembly's prayerful response in song is encouraged. When presence, bearing, and attitude affirm that sung prayer is truly prayer, then common song will be taken seriously and entered into unhesitantly.

When fulfilling the role of psalmist the cantor partakes in a common ministry with the reader, the proclaimer of the gospel, and the homilist: all are heralds of God's living word. This oneness of purpose is apparent during the liturgy of the word when all these ministers share, or at least may share, the ambo which represents the uniqueness and dignity of the salvific word. The psalmody following the reading is an expression of the reception of God's word. But it is not private meditation or private prayer. Rather, it is an action of the community which raises its voice in sung prayer as it makes the songs of the Bible its own, as it responds to God's word with God's word. As in all psalmody, attention to the text is of critical importance for the psalmist. Care must be given to enunciation and diction. Of no less consequence is the ability and desire to communicate that vast spectrum of emotions, moods, and feelings reflected in the sacred texts. Musical artistry and joyous enthusiasm certainly contribute in no small measure to the success of this endeavor. But above all else there must be a personal conviction that the psalmist is the bearer of God present and speaking in the text that is sung. The lyrical outpourings of praise, thanksgiving, and petition must first be appropriated by the psalmist before they can be experienced as prayer by the assembly. St. John Chrysostom's exhortation to the people regarding their sung refrains to the psalms is also applicable to the psalmist: "Your voice proclaims that you love him above everything, that you prefer nothing to him, that you burn with love for him" (*Expositio in Psalmum* 41:5).

The cantor is often called upon to sing psalmody and similar structural forms at other times, e.g., during the entrance procession, during the collection and preparation of the gifts, and during the distribution of the eucharist. Frequently the cantor will lead acclamations, litanies, and even hymns. The cantorial role is further extended on those occasions when no choir is present. Often the responsibility of teaching new music or, when necessary, rehearsing old music is entrusted to the cantor. In some communities the cantor acts as an "animator," as one who energizes by providing a spirit of vitality and unity to the celebration. The cantor as animator may check the physical details of the music (e.g., microphones and folders) before the people arrive, welcome the assembly, spiritually prepare its members for sung prayer, give necessary directions during the liturgy, and help regulate the rhythm of the assembly's sung, spoken, and silent prayer. Whatever the task assigned—whether during the eucharist, the celebration of the other sacraments, the liturgy of the hours—the cantor never distracts from the prayerfulness of the occasion. Attention to the nature of ritual action with its interplay of elements and particular ministries is required. Always avoided are verbosity, explanations, and tutorial attitudes. The cantor is a discreet servant enabling the assembly to express in song its own prayer.

Suggested Questions for Discussion

1. What personal qualities and technical skills should a cantor possess? How would you rank them?
2. How does the role of the cantor differ from that of the psalmist?

3. What is the difference between a cantor and a leader of song? Are both needed?
4. What is the difference between a cantor and a cantor-animator? What special qualities or skills are required for the animator role?
5. What are the advantages and/or disadvantages of the cantor wearing a distinctive garb?
6. What methods of recruiting cantors have proven successful in your community?
7. What type of formation is given to cantors in your community? Musical? Spiritual? Liturgical? How often?
8. On what liturgical occasions does the cantor minister in your community? Why are these occasions selected? What possibilities exist for extending this ministry to other celebrations?
9. What have you found to be the best physical location for the cantor in your assembly? Why?

Bibliography

Bauman, William A. *The Ministry of Music: A Guide for the Practicing Church Musician.* 2nd edition. Ed. by Elaine Rendler and Thomas Fuller. Washington, D.C.: The Liturgical Conference, 1979. pp. 31-46.

Blain, Laetitia. "The Cantor's Performance: Competent, Prayerful, Well Prepared." *Pastoral Music* 3:2 (December-January 1979), pp. 24-26.

Butler, Richard. "The Church Musician in History." *Pastoral Music* 3:3 (February-March 1979), pp. 12-13.

Chicago Liturgy Training Publications. *Cantors and Leaders of Song: A Workshop.* 3 cassette tapes.

Colbert, Annick. "The Animator Communicates the Fervor of Life." *Pastoral Music* 4:1 (October-November 1979), pp. 26-28.

Connolly, Michael. *The Parish Cantor: Helping Catholics Pray in Song.* Old Hickory, Tennessee: Pastoral Arts Associates of North America, 1982.

Conry, Tom. "Is Animation Just Another Fad?" *Pastoral Music* 4:1 (October-November 1979), pp. 48-49.

Corbin, S. "Cantor in Christian Liturgy." *New Catholic Encyclopedia* III, p. 71.

Deiss, Lucien. *Persons in Liturgical Celebrations*, pp. 42-44.

Deiss, Lucien. *Spirit and Song of the New Liturgy*, pp. 47-62.

Foley, Edward. "The Cantor in Historical Perspective." *Worship* 56:3 (May 1982), pp. 194-213.

Fragomeni, Richard. "The Animator Is a Whirlwind . . . The Illusion Is that the Animator Is Stationary." *Pastoral Music* 4:1 (October-November 1979), pp. 23-25.

Gelineau, Joseph. "The Animator." *Pastoral Music* 4:1 (October-November 1979), pp. 19-22. Reprinted in *Pastoral Music in Prac-*

tice. Ed. by Virgil C. Funk and Gabe Huck. pp. 35-41.

Gelineau, Joseph. *Voices and Instruments in Christian Worship*, pp. 77-80.

Hartgen, William. "For Musicians." *Touchstones for Liturgical Ministers*. Ed. by Virginia Sloyan. pp. 23-26.

Neuchterlein, Herbert. "Cantor." *Key Words in Church Music*. Ed. by Carl Schalk. St. Louis: Concordia Publishing House, 1978. pp. 45-47.

Patterson, Vincent. "The Cantor: From Soloist to Song Leader." *Pastoral Music* 2:4 (April-May 1978), pp. 23-25.

Stratman, Tom. "The Animating Cantor." *Pastoral Music* 4:1 (October-November 1979), pp. 14-15.

Wojcik, Richard J. *The Cantor: Changing Words to Song and Prayer*. Kansas City, Missouri: National Catholic Reporter Publishing Company. Cassette.

5

Choir

5
Choir

Historical Background

The unisonous singing of the whole assembly was considered a
special sign of unity in the early Church. Gathering together each
morning and evening and especially on the Lord's Day, the community
raised one voice as its members joyfully expressed their shared faith
through hymns and acclamations. They responded to the chanting of
the psalms and at times alternated in a simple form of antiphonal
psalmody. In spite of this deep attachment to the unifying power of
common song, two special groups of singers, i.e., those of women and
of boys, appeared toward the end of the fourth century. Each would
have its own destiny.

Special choirs of women played a prominent role in Greek and
Roman religions where they participated in religious processions and
in the offering of sacrifices to the gods. Female choirs are also found in
the Old Testament (cfr. Exodus 15:20-21 and Judges 21:21). But their
first appearance in Christian worship sprang from the desire of certain
heretics to attract more followers.[1] These efforts must have proved
successful since St. Ephraem (c.303-373) in Syria established choirs of
consecrated virgins to counteract the allurement posed by the use of
female singers in heterodox groups. The saint even personally instructed these Christian women in the art of psalmody. There is also
evidence to suggest that other eastern bishops reacted in a similar vein
to the attraction posed by heretical worship practices. We know, for
example, that in the East it was customary for virgins to gather in
church for the singing of psalmody. Some bishops, however, not con-
curring with Ephraem's pastoral approach, completely rejected an im-

itation of heretical innovations: eventually they even extended their opposition to women singing as members of the assembly at large. Yet in spite of such local resistance, women continued to sing in their own religious communities, as part of the local assembly, and to a lesser extent even as a special singing group within the assembly. But another group of singers, namely the boy choir, was also evolving. It encountered no ecclesiastical opposition, and in the end seems to have not only replaced the female choir but also played some role in the decline of the assembly's common song.

The religions of both Greece and Rome cultivated singing by boys since the pure vocal quality of the unchanged male voice was considered as having a special efficacy upon the deities. Starting with the fourth century the use of boys as special groups of singers appeared within Christian worship. Egeria's description of the late fourth century liturgy in Jerusalem mentions young boys responding Kyrie eleison to a litany led by the deacon.[2] The *Testamentum Domini*, a treatise originally written in Greek during the fourth or fifth century, speaks of boys joining the virgins in responding to a cantor, alternating with the virgins in chanting the psalmody at the daily hours, and singing the Vesper canticles to which the people responded Alleluia.[3] In the latter case, no doubt an instance of responsorial psalmody, the boys were substituting for the cantor. We also find reference to a special group of boy singers in the West. The *Expositio Liturgicae Gallicanae*, a work attributed by some to St. Germanus of Paris (c.496-576), mentions that boys sing the Kyrie eleison at the beginning of Mass.[4] Although details are sketchy, there is reason to believe that the development of the boy choir was somehow related to the progressive use of young males as readers.[5] These youths were trained not only in reading but also in singing. Their musical formation may have been accelerated to offset the use of boy choirs among certain heretical groups such as the Nestorians. Such primitive "schools" of young readers and singers, gathered together under the aegis of monks or secular clergy, probably were the forerunners of such subsequent and more formal groups as the Roman schola cantorum.

A number of factors may have contributed to the emergence of special groups of liturgical singers. Beginning with the early fourth century the Church's liturgy underwent a dramatic transformation. No longer a small and marginal group which was often the object of persecution, the Christian community was now given the freedom to expand its liturgical and musical forms. More opportunity was provided to enhance the basic patterns of its ritual life. For example, many elements of imperial ceremony (e.g., incense, candles, insignia, vesture) entered the liturgy by way of the bishop who was considered akin to a civil official. Just as the arrival of the Roman emperor was accompanied by song, so singing came to attend the entrance of the bishop. Formerly the community gathered in smaller houses and buildings. Now, as the numbers of the faithful increased, the assembly congregated in larger edifices which fostered the use of dramatic elements. There was a psychological need to utilize the new space, and formal processions of ministers and people were soon to evolve. But since the ministers and at times the faithful themselves participated in these processions, the task of providing a musical accompaniment to fill up the time of the movement was entrusted to a group of specialized singers. At Rome the most celebrated group of such musicians was the schola cantorum.

The origins of the Roman schola are obscure. According to John the Deacon who wrote about 872, it was Pope Gregory I (590-604) who established the schola by providing some estates to defray its expenses and by constructing two dwellings, one at the foot of St. Peter's and the other in the vicinity of the Lateran basilica, to house its members.[6] If John's account is correct, the purpose of this double branched college of cantors may well have been to provide music for the schedule of daily Masses organized at Rome by Gregory. Others, however, honor Pope Vitalian (657-672) as the founder of the papal schola.[7] Although most scholars tend to view the schola's establishment toward the middle of the seventh century, an attempt has been made to reconcile these two traditions.[8] In this hypothesis Pope Vitalian merely created a papal schola out of the Lateran center, and it is from this group, which altered the ancient chant to reflect the increasing splendor of papal celebrations, that our present Gregorian repertoire originates.

Whatever its origins, the structure of the schola was certainly well organized by the end of the seventh century. Its leader, a subdeacon, was called the *precentor* or *prior scholae*. He supervised the details of the readings and chants of the Mass, helped the pope vest, and gave the intonations for the chants. The *precentor* was assisted by three other subdeacons, i.e., the *secundus*, the *tertius*, and the *quartus*. The latter, also called the archcantor, was the music teacher of the acolytes, other clerics, and choir boys who formed the body of the schola. He also traveled abroad as an apostle of the Roman method of singing. Bede, for example, writing about 730, says that John the Archcantor was brought to England in 678 as an official pedagogue of the Roman chant.[9]

During the papal Mass of the late seventh century the members of the schola, arranged in two double rows facing each other at the entrance to the sanctuary, were primarily entrusted with the psalmatic chants that accompanied the entrance of the ministers, the collection and preparation of the gifts, and the distribution of the eucharist. Although there is much evidence that the Ordinary chants of the Mass were initially sung by the assembly, in the late seventh century papal Mass the schola sang or at least intoned the Kyrie and the Agnus Dei.[10]

The Roman schola cantorum served as a model for similar groups in cathedrals and monasteries throughout western Europe. Often under the direct tutelage of Roman instructors, renowned singing schools evolved in such cities as Metz, Chartres, and Soisson. Many of the young choristers entered into the ranks of the ordained clergy or took religious vows. But as musical notation became widespread, there was less necessity for the concentrated and protracted memorization required by an oral tradition of learning the chant. This would play a significant role in the eventual decline of the singing school.

Complementing the schola was another though less formal group of singers, i.e., the chorus of assisting clergy. Already in the late seventh century papal Mass the singing of the Sanctus was assigned to the subdeacons who themselves may have been members of the schola. Although a great diversity of musical practice existed during the Middle Ages, there is evidence that the clerics serving as ministers of the presiding bishop were gradually assuming various sung parts of the Ordinary. These chants, once sung by the whole assembly, little by little were becoming the prerogative of clergy alone.

Other than in monastic circles, the choir of the pre-Renaissance period was a small group of singers often composed of a few clerics and in some places young boys destined for holy orders. As new musical techniques were progressively applied to the traditional chant, a change occurred in the accustomed manner of singing. A small ensemble of solo voices alternated with the chorus singing in unison. As the emerging polyphonic style was extended to the whole liturgical text, laymen capable of handling the intricacies of the new music gradually replaced the assisting clergy and the old schola. Yet it was only in the fifteenth century that more than one singer to a part become common. But even at this time the choir remained a small body with its members all singing from a single score or choir book. It was only in the Baroque era that massive choirs appeared in some of the larger churches. Since female voices were excluded from liturgical choirs till the seventeenth century, castrati were used in Italy. Having the lungs and chest of an adult as well as the larynx of a youth, these singers were in great demand since they possessed both wide range and great power in addition to the unique tonal quality of the male soprano voice.

The future history of the choir generally mirrored the development of music and the understanding of liturgy current at the time. Large choirs, common in cathedrals and major churches, often employed professional singers who performed the works of contemporary or past masters. In smaller churches amateur singers were the rule. Particular repertoire varied, according to the talents of individual choirs, from concert pieces to more simple compositions, the latter often written in poor imitation of the major composers. Generally emphasis was placed on settings of the Ordinary. Although Caecilianism in the late nineteenth century and Pope Pius X's 1903 motu proprio *Tra le sollicitudini* attempted, certainly with some measure of success, to reform the choral repertoire, the choir remained primarily a performing group whose function was considered that of enriching and ennobling the liturgy through music.

The history of the choir witnesses an interesting evolution of the interrelationships between its function, membership, and location. In its origin and early medieval development the schola was a male and often clerical institution. It was located in close proximity to both the people and the clergy, often immediately in front of the chancel but also at times within it. But once laics began to replace the clergy, there arose a problem since the laity were forbidden entrance into the chancel, a prescription found as early as the Second Synod of Tours in 567.[11] Consequently the choir had to be transferred elsewhere. Often this was in the jube, a small gallery above and aside the rood screen, i.e., a wall which separated the chancel from the nave and upon which was located a cross (rood). As the size of the choir increased, it was further separated from the assembly in a gallery or tribune surrounding the chancel. But memories of clerical origins perdured. Since the liturgy was considered a clerical action, only male voices were allowed. It was not till the seventeenth century, when musical demands were more exacting than formerly, that female voices were admitted. This was also a period when the organ, increasing in size, was being used to accompany the singing. Accordingly, the choir was moved to a gallery in the rear of the church where the organ was located. Here, separated from both altar and people, the role of the choir as a performing organization solidified. People even turned around during Mass to look at the singers. To offset this abuse some attempts were made in the nineteenth century to place the choir in a tribune at the side of the altar or in another place which concealed the singers. Generally, however, the choir remained in the rear above the main entrance to the church.

To some extent the presence of women in the choir was indicative of the concert and theatrical idiom characteristic of much nineteenth century liturgical music. Pope Pius X in his 1903 motu proprio reacted against such compositions and insisted on the sacred character of liturgical music and on the liturgical role of the choir. Mindful of the clerical beginnings of the choir, the Pope stated that "liturgical singing belongs properly to the choir of clerics; wherefore singers in church, if they are laymen, are the substitutes of the ecclesiastical choir . . . . It follows from the same principle that the singers in church have a real liturgical office, and that women, therefore, being incapable of such an office, cannot be admitted to the choir" (n.12-13).[12] In their pastoral wisdom most bishops simply overlooked this prohibition or made subtle distinctions. It was not till the 1955 encyclical *Musicae sacrae disciplina* of Pope Pius XII that women, in the absence of boy singers, were officially and generally permitted to be members of the choir, provided that they were separated from the men and that the choir itself was located outside the sanctuary area.

51

The reforms of Vatican II consider the choir as part of the assembly and hence there is no restriction on its membership. Its location should be such that its function of singing on behalf of, to, and with the assembly be clearly apparent.

Documentation

Constitution on the Sacred Liturgy

29. . . . members of the choir also exercise a genuine liturgical function. They ought, therefore, to discharge their office with the sincere piety and decorum demanded by so exalted a ministry and rightly expected of them by God's people. Consequently they must all be deeply imbued with the spirit of the liturgy, each in his own measure, and they must be trained to perform their functions in a correct and orderly manner.

114. Choirs must be diligently promoted, especially in cathedral churches; but bishops and other pastors of souls must be at pains to ensure that, whenever the sacred action is celebrated with song, the whole body of the faithful may be able to contribute that active participation which is rightly theirs, as laid down in Art. 28 and 30.

Instruction for the Proper Implementation of the Constitution on the Sacred Liturgy

97. The places for the schola and the organ shall be so arranged that it will be clearly evident that the singers and the organist form a part of the united community of the faithful so that they may fulfill their liturgical functions more suitably.

Instruction on Music in the Liturgy

19. Because of the liturgical ministry it performs, the choir—or the *Capella musica*, or *schola cantorum*—deserves particular mention. Its role has become something of yet greater importance and weight by reason of the norms of the Council concerning the liturgical renewal. Its duty is, in effect, to insure the proper performance of the parts which belong to it, according to the different kinds of music sung, and to encourage the active participation of the faithful in the singing. Therefore:
a) There should be choirs, or *Capellae*, or *scholae cantorum*, especially in cathedrals and other major churches, in seminaries and religious houses of studies, and they should be carefully encouraged.
b) It would also be desirable for similar choirs to be set up in smaller churches.
20. Large choirs (*Capellae musicae*) existing in basilicas, cathedrals, monasteries and other major churches, which have in the course of centuries earned for themselves high renown by preserving and developing a musical heritage of inestimable value, should be retained

for sacred celebrations of a more elaborate kind, according to their own traditional norms, recognized and approved by the Ordinary. However, the directors of these choirs and the rectors of the churches should take care that the people always associate themselves with the singing by performing at least the easier sections of those parts which belong to them.

22. The choir can consist, according to the customs of each country and other circumstances, of either men and boys, or men and boys only, or men and women, or even, where there is a genuine case for it, of women only.

23. Taking into account the layout of each church, the choir should be placed in such a way:
a) That its nature should be clearly apparent—namely that it is a part of the whole congregation, and that it fulfills a special role;
b) That it is easier for it to fulfill its liturgical function;
c) That each of its members may be able to participate easily in the Mass, that is to say by sacramental participation.
Whenever the choir also includes women, it should be placed outside the sanctuary (*presbyterium*).

24. Besides musical formation, suitable liturgical and spiritual formation must also be given to the members of the choir, in such a way that the proper performance of their liturgical role will not only enhance the beauty of the celebration and be an excellent example for the faithful, but will bring spiritual benefit to the choir-members themselves.

General Instruction of the Roman Missal

63. The schola or choir exercises a liturgical function. It sings the different parts proper to it and encourages active participation of the people in singing.

274. The choir forms part of the assembled faithful, but it has a special function and should be so located that its nature may be clearly apparent. Its location should facilitate the exercise of its function and the full sacramental participation of its members.

Music in Catholic Worship

36. A well-trained choir adds beauty and solemnity to the liturgy and also assists and encourages the singing of the congregation. The Second Vatican Council, in speaking of the choir, stated emphatically: "Choirs must be diligently promoted," provided that "the whole body of the faithful may be able to contribute that active participation which is rightly theirs."
"At times the choir, within the congregation of the faithful and as part of it, will assume the role of leadership, while at other times it will retain its own distinctive ministry. This means that the choir will lead

the people in sung prayer, by alternating or reinforcing the sacred song of the congregation, or by enhancing it with the addition of a musical elaboration. At other times in the course of liturgical celebration the choir alone will sing works whose musical demands enlist and challenge its competence."

38. The *proper placing* of an organ and choir according to the arrangement and accoustics of the church will facilitate celebration. Practically speaking, the choir must be near the director and the organ (both console and sound). The choir ought to be able to perform without too much distraction; the acoustics ought to give a lively presence of sound in the choir area and allow both tone and word to reach the congregation with clarity. Visually it is desirable that the choir appear to be part of the worshiping community, yet a part which serves in a unique way.

Environment and Art in Catholic Worship

83. Because choir, instrumentalists and organ often function as an ensemble, they need to be located together in such a way that the organist can see the other musicians and the liturgical action directly or by means of a simple mirror.

Reflection

The years immediately following the Second Vatican Council were torturous times for many. A community which for centuries had few built-in mechanisms for dealing with change was being asked to renew its life and move in directions which, within recent memory, were unknown and even considered perilous by some. It was predictable, at least in retrospect, that the musical life of the Church would also undergo profound trauma. The problem was especially acute for many choir directors and members. With the introduction of the vernacular liturgy, much of the choir's traditional repertoire was simply outdated. Furthermore, in spite of reminders to the contrary, the emphasis on the singing of the assembly was interpreted as challenging the very existence of the choir. Accentuating the difficulty was the appearance of the folk singer who, for centuries relegated to the fringes of the Church's song but now assuming a very visible role within the liturgy, was perceived to be in competition with the parish choir. As a result of these and other tensions, some choirs were immediately disbanded; others gradually faded away as doubts regarding their liturgical role remained unresolved. Those that survived often experienced the pains of change and adjustment.

Much has happened since those turbulent years. Today the Roman Church is experiencing something akin to the beginnings of a renaissance of choral singing. As always, the choir remains a group of trained and rehearsed singers, but its art is no longer to add, like frosting on the cake, a layer of solemnity and dignity to the liturgical action. It is no longer a musical organization performing to an audience. Choir members now enjoy a new vision of themselves, being aware that their role is not only important but is as challenging as it is demanding. They understand that they are members of the assembly, yet members who serve that assembly and its common prayer through the sublime art of music. No longer located in a distant loft or gallery, the choir takes its rightful place among the people, and its musical talents are to energize the worship of this people. When the prayer of the community is led, enhanced, and inspired by the beauty of choral singing, then the experience of this prayer attains the highest peaks of expressing communion with God and others. It is not without reason that in the Byzantine tradition the choir is pictured as representing "the heavenly powers." This presumes, of course, that the choir can sing well: good intentions are never any substitute for true artistry, for accomplished musicianship.

Determining the precise function of the choir hinges not only upon its fundamental role as a servant, but also upon such variables as the type of celebration and the nature of its structural components. Obviously the choir, as part of the assembly, joins the people in singing those parts of the celebration which by their very nature always belong to the congregation, e.g., responses and acclamations. Common song is thereby stimulated, reinforced, and sustained. In fact, the quality and enthusiasm of the assembly's singing is often a reflection of the quality and enthusiasm of the choir's participation. The choir can also enrich the assembly's song. Familiar music of all kinds can be given a new sound through the use of harmony and descants. The choir alternating with the assembly gives a new dimension to common song. Furthermore, there are moments when the choir, singing alone, makes its particular contribution to the prayer of the people, e.g., before or after the liturgy, during the preparation of the gifts. At such times some of the Latin repertoire of the past might still serve to enhance the emotive quality of the celebration. On special occasions the choir might also sing certain chants which ordinarily belong to the assembly, e.g., songs to accompany processions, and hymns like Gloria. The choir's service, in the final analysis, is not determined by its repertoire, by the music it knows. Rather, it is the flow and mood of the celebration, the equilibrium of its roles and parts, which indicate how the choir may best serve the prayer of the assembly.

In many parishes there are two, sometimes even more, choral groups, e.g., traditional choir, folk choir, children's choir. In the recent past a sometimes subtle, sometimes outspoken, rivalry existed between the traditional and the folk choir. The mere existence of the one seemed to threaten the self-image of the other. Today, however, there is a growing interrelationship between choral groups. Often there is a broadening and sharing of accustomed repertoires. Some communities unite resources in certain major celebrations, not by alternating or dividing musical selections in ping-pong fashion, but by combining, when possible, voices and instruments in the same selections. This is an indication of maturity. It is an effective sign to singers and assembly alike that all choirs share a commonality of service to the community at prayer.

Suggested Questions for Discussion

1. What factors determine the musical role of the choir in a particular celebration?
2. What qualities should a choir director look for in recruiting new members?
3. Should sharing a common faith be a consideration in accepting new members?
4. To what extent should choir members be educated liturgically that they might better understand their role as well as decisions made regarding choice and position of musical selections?
5. Do you recommend a distinct garb for choir members?
6. What criteria determine decisions regarding the physical location of the choir?
7. What role should the choir director play in the liturgical planning process?
8. What approaches do you recommend to a parish for reconciling various choral groups that are antagonistic toward one another?
9. On what liturgical occasions do choirs minister in your comunity? What possibilities exist for extending this ministry to other celebrations?

Bibliography

Bauman, William A. *The Ministry of Music: A Guide for the Practicing Church Musician.* 2nd edition. pp.47-58.

Braun, H. Myron. *What Every Choir Member Should Know.* Old Hickory, Tennessee: Pastoral Arts Associates, 1982.

Cunningham, W. Patrick. "Do Parish Choirs Have a Future?" *Today's Parish* 10:5 (May-June 1978), pp.38-40.

Cunningham, W. Patrick. "New Life for the Parish Choir." *Homiletic and Pastoral Review* 74:10 (July 1974), pp.29-32.

Deiss, Lucien. *Persons in Liturgical Celebrations,* pp.35-42, 47-49.

Deiss, Lucien. *Spirit and Song of the New Liturgy,* pp.37-46.

Gelineau, Joseph. *Voices and Instruments in Christian Worship,* pp.84-89.

Gnader, Marie. "Discipline, Technique, Artistry: Tips to Choir Performance." *Pastoral Music* 3:2 (December-January 1979), pp.22-23.

Hartgen, William. "For Musicians." *Touchstones for Liturgical Ministers.* Ed. by Virginia Sloyan. pp.23-26.

Hucke, Helmut. "Schola Cantorum." *New Catholic Encyclopedia* XII, p.1143.

Johns, Donald. "Choir, History." *Key Words in Church Music.* Ed. by Carl Schalk. pp.64-69.

Kosnik, James. "The Choir's Role at Eucharist." *Pastoral Music* 3:6 (August-September 1979), pp.15-16.

Krisman, Ronald. "Even if You Can't Sing . . . You Need a Choir." *Pastoral Music* 3:6 (August-September 1979), pp.17-19.

Lambert, Paul. "There's More to Choir than Singing." *Pastoral Music* 3:6 (August-September 1979), pp.30-33.

Kovalevsky, Maxime. "The Role of the Choir in Christian Liturgy." *Roles in the Liturgical Assembly,* by A.M. Triaca and others. New York: Pueblo Publishing Company, 1981. pp.193-206.

McGrath, Roberta. "Effective Music Ministry." *Today's Parish* 12:3 (March 1980), pp.24-26.

Peloquin, C. Alexander and Rembert G. Weakland. "Choir." *New Catholic Encyclopedia* III, pp.621-622.

Pfeil, Elmer. "All the King's Horses . . ." *Pastoral Music* 2:4 (April-May 1978), pp.26-29.

Robinson, J.K. "Starting a Parish Choir." *Pastoral Music* 3:6 (August-September 1979), pp.24-26.

Wozniak, Joseph. "What Ever Happened to the Choir?" *Pastoral Music* 3:6 (August-September 1979), pp.21-23.

6

Instrumentalists

6
Instrumentalists

Historical Background

The use of musical instruments was deeply ingrained in the artistic tradition of the Jewish people. In daily life, at the royal court, and especially in the temple liturgy, musical instruments were employed to provide solo music and to accompany the singing of the people. Certain instruments, such as trumpets and horns, were reserved to the priests, their use being ascribed to divine command: "It is the sons of Aaron, the priests, who shall blow the trumpets, and the use of these is prescribed by perpetual statute for you and your descendants" (Numbers 10:8). The Levites were also assigned their own particular instruments by divine decree, for we read in the Second Book of Chronicles that King Hezekiah "stationed the Levites in the Lord's house with cymbals, harps, and lyres according to the prescriptions of David, of Gad the king's seer, and of Nathan the prophet; for the prescriptions were from the Lord through his prophets" (29:25). Percussive instruments such as bells and tambourines served to enhance the singing of the people. Then there were flutes, pipes, and all types of wind instruments that could be played by all and were commonly used on various social occasions.

Christian worship, receiving more from the rituals of the Jewish home and synogogue than from those of the temple, did not inherit this tradition of instrumental music. Although the playing of certain string instruments did at times occur at certain religious meals and at popular feasts, the Fathers of the Church were of one mind in completely excluding instrumental music from the liturgical assembly.[1]

61

Underlying this prohibition were two major concerns, one cultural and the other theological.

In ancient Greece and Rome instrumental music was closely associated with pagan sacrifices, offerings of incense, drink libations, and the celebration of popular religious feasts. Greek cultic practice employed many types of string, wind, and percussive instruments. At Rome the flute predominated. Instrumentalists were to ward off whatever was considered detrimental to the devotion of the worshipers and to induce a feeling of ecstacy among the adherents of the cults. Anxious to avoid the appearance of any compromise with pagan practices and knowing how easy it remained for the recently baptized to succumb to the allurements of their former way of life, the Church for centuries totally rejected the use of musical instruments in its liturgy. The prayer of the assembly was to be vocal prayer, expressing the yearnings of the human heart and not the neutral and impersonal sound of an instrument. To make this point the Fathers often recalled that it was the human voice singing psalms and hymns which had replaced those instruments so common in pagan worship.[2] But instruments were not only used by the pagans for cultic purposes. In Rome and elsewhere instrumentalists were also called upon to play at private gatherings such as banquets. Many of these were notorious for their excesses and debauchery. Despite this association, a few writers were somewhat tolerant of the private use of instruments, especially the lyre and cithara.[3]

Of equal concern to the Fathers was the preservation of the liturgical assembly's one voice raised in common song. To weaken that voice in any way was to weaken the unity and harmony of the people gathered to pray. But to introduce instrumental music into the liturgy would diminish the strength of the assembly's unisonous voice: it would be to divide the oneness of song coming from a single body.

Yet the Fathers could not ignore the Judaic tradition of using instrumental music within cult. They had to explain to the faithful why the Old Testament approved of instrumental music within the liturgy. The Fathers sought refuge in that passage of Amos which rejected external worship without inner truth: "Away with your noisy songs! I will not listen to the melodies of your harps" (5:23). In the patristic perspective God was not really pleased with Jewish instrumental music but merely allowed it as a concession to the weakness of the Israelites who were surrounded on all sides by pagan worship. It was simply tolerated to help the Jewish people overcome their attraction to the idol worship practiced by their neighbors. In the words of Theodoret of Cyr (c.393-c.466), it was merely a "lesser evil to prevent a greater one."[4]

In their attempt to explain ancient Jewish practice and to offer a substitute for the use of instruments among the pagans, the Fathers took great delight in endowing the various instruments with allegorical meanings. Origen (c.185-c.254), for instance, considered the trumpet as representing the word of God, cymbals as standing for the soul in love with God, etc.[5] Eusebius (c.260-340), bishop of Caesaria, wrote that "our cithara is the whole body, by whose movement and action the soul sings a fitting hymn to God, and our ten-stringed psaltery is the veneration of the Holy Spirit by the five senses of the body and the five virtues of the spirit."[6]

Although this spiritualization of musical instruments continued down to the early Middle Ages, there is no reason to believe that instruments, other than eventually the organ, were employed during the liturgical offices. For centuries the music of the Church was vocal and unisonous. It was only with the emergence and development of polyphony that various types of musical instruments were introduced within the liturgy, Already in the thirteenth century, according to many scholars, instruments supplied for or doubled certain choral parts, e.g., the tenor line in the motet. Yet it was especially during the Baroque period that instrumental music blossomed. Composers wrote for small ensembles of string, wind, and brass instruments and their various combinations. Recital pieces such as the church sonata were performed not only at sacred concerts but also during Mass and Vespers. Instrumental accompaniment to choral singing, a distinguishing mark of the Venetian composers, eventually reached gigantic proportions. Orazio Benevoli (1605-1672), for example, wrote a fifty-three part Mass (two 8 part choirs, two string ensembles, two ensembles of wind instruments, and two ensembles of brass) for the consecration of the Salzburg cathedral in 1628. Other composers expanded Mass and motet texts to form regular cantatas comprised of solos, choral passages, and instrumental introductions and interludes.

Starting with the Classical period it was the orchestral style which dominated the composition of liturgical music. Though a few composers preferred the a capella idiom of the past, the majority merely applied to the liturgical texts the orchestral techniques and principles that proved so successful in the symphonic writing of the time. Striking examples are the Masses and other religious compositions of Franz Joseph Haydn (1732-1809) and Wolfgang Amadeus Mozart (1756-1791). The liturgy often became the setting for purely instrumental selections such as Mozart's *Epistle Sonatas* which were meant to be performed between the epistle and gospel at Mass. Major churches employed as part of their musical staff not only singers and organists but also other instrumentalists. Instrumental accompaniment for the choir's singing became an accepted practice throughout most of western Europe. Even those reform musicians of the late nineteenth century who espoused the Renaissance a capella style as the ideal for liturgical music simply followed contemporary practice and did not hesitate to utilize orchestral instruments to accompany much of their choral writing for the liturgy.

In light of the conservative nature of the Roman liturgy, it is surprising that the transition from a vocal to a vocal-instrumental idiom encountered little opposition. St. Thomas Aquinas (1225-1274), living at a time when the use of instruments in liturgy was still infrequent, merely stated that the instruments of the Old Testament are excluded from the Church because they appeal to the emotions rather than form "good interior dispositions."[7] A more favorable judgment, perhaps the result of developing performance practices, was that of St. Antonius (1389-1459), the archbishop of Florence, who mentions in his *Summa* that "organs and other instruments began to be fruitfully used for the praise of God by the Prophet David."[8] Influential theologians such as Thomas Cajetan (1469-1543), Robert Bellarmine (1542-1621), and Francisco Suarez (1548-1617), approved or at least permitted the growing usage.[9] On the other hand, St. Charles Borromeo at the Council of Milan in 1565 prohibited all instruments other than the organ.[10] Opposition was much greater among certain Protestant Reformers. Zwingli (1484-1531), for example, completely eliminated all music from worship, and John Calvin (1501-1564) rejected all instruments as "childish elements" for which Christians have no need.[11]

Although instrumental music in church was a natural and generally accepted partner of the developing art of music, a certain tension long remained between the Church and the use of orchestral instruments. The problem was not the patristic concern that instrumental music would disrupt the common song of the assembly. Indeed the musical participation of the people in the liturgy had long disappeared. But the Fathers also rejected instrumental music because of its pagan connotations. It was this question of association, now with the music of the theater, that occasioned the ecclesiastical apprehension evident in numerous Roman documents. An example is the encyclical *Annus qui* by Pope Benedict XIV (1740-1758). In an attempt to eliminate the use of theatrical music from the church, the Pope divided various instruments into those that were suitable and those that were unsuitable. Permitted were the organ, "the tuba, the large and small tetrachord, the flutes, the lyres and the lute, provided they serve to strengthen and support the voices." Excluded were "tambourines, cors da classe, trumpets, harps, guitars, and in general all instruments that give a theatrical swing to the music."[12] During nineteenth century Rome, where the tradition of unaccompanied singing was very strong, written permission had to be obtained from either the pope or his vicar-general before even the approved instruments could be used. In 1903 Pope Pius X also required the bishop's approval for the use of instruments. These, however, were merely "tolerated," and always forbidden were the piano and "all noisy or irreverent instruments such as drums, kettledrums, cymbals, triangles and so on."[13]

As the liturgical reforms initiated by Pius X and others began to bear fruit and as the theatrical style became less common, a more tolerant attitude toward instruments appeared. This is evident in Pope Pius XII's encyclical of December 25, 1955, *Musicae sacrae disciplina*, which endorsed the use of instruments, especially the strings: "Besides the organ, other instruments can be called upon to give great help in attaining the lofty purpose of sacred music, so long as they play nothing profane, nothing clamorous or strident and nothing at variance with the sacred services or the dignity of the place. Among these the violin and other musical instruments that use the bow are outstanding because, when they are played by themselves or with other stringed instruments or with the organ, they express the joyous and sad sentiments of the soul with indescribable power."[14] While refraining from such accolades, the Fathers at Vatican II simply left the use of instruments to the discretion of the competent territorial bodies of bishops. No specific instruments were excluded provided that they "accord with the dignity of the temple, and that they truly contribute to the edification of the faithful" (n.120).

Documentation

Constitution on the Sacred Liturgy

120 . . . other instruments also may be admitted for use in divine worship, with the knowledge and consent of the competent territorial authority, as laid down in Art. 22:2, 37, and 40. This may be done, however, only on condition that the instruments are suitable, or can be made suitable, for sacred use, in accord with the dignity of the temple, and truly contribute to the edification of the faithful.

Instruction on Music in the Liturgy

62. Musical instruments can be very useful in sacred celebrations, whether they accompany the singing or whether they are played as solo instruments. "The pipe organ is to be held in high esteem . . . ." "The use of other instruments may also be admitted in divine worship, given the decision and consent of the competent territorial authority, provided that the instruments are suitable for sacred use, or can be adapted to it, that they are in keeping with the dignity of the temple, and truly contribute to the edification of the faithful."

63. In permitting and using musical instruments, the culture and traditions of individual peoples must be taken into account. However, those instruments which are, by common opinion and use, suitable for secular music only, are to be altogether prohibited from every liturgical celebration and from popular devotions. Any musical instrument permitted in divine worship should be used in such a way that it meets the needs of the liturgical celebration, and is in the interests both of the beauty of worship and the edification of the faithful.

64. The use of musical instruments to accompany the singing can act as a support to the voices, render participation easier, and achieve a deeper union in the assembly. However, their sound should not so

overwhelm the voices that it is difficult to make out the text; and when some part is proclaimed aloud by the priest or a minister by virtue of his role, they should be silent.

65. In sung or said Masses, the organ, or other instruments legitimately admitted, can be used to accompany the singing of the choir and the people; it can also be played solo at the beginning before the priest reaches the altar, at the Offertory, at the Communion, and at the end of Mass. The same rule, with the necessary adaptations, can be applied to other sacred celebrations.

66. The playing of these same instruments as solos is not permitted in Advent, Lent, during the Sacred Triduum and in the Offices and Masses of the Dead.

67. It is highly desirable that organists and other musicians should not only possess the skill to play properly the instrument entrusted to them: they should also enter into and be thoroughly aware of the spirit of the liturgy, so that even when playing *ex tempore*, they will enrich the sacred celebration according to the true nature of each of its parts, and encourage the participation of the faithful.

General Instruction of the Roman Missal

275. The organ and other approved musical instruments should be located in a suitable place so that they can assist both choir and people when they are singing and can be heard properly when played alone.

Third Instruction on the Correct Implementation of the Constitution on the Sacred Liturgy

3c. Attention should be given to the choice of musical instruments: these should be few in number, suited to the place and the community, should favor prayer and not be too loud.

Music in Catholic Worship

37. In the dioceses of the United States, "musical instruments other than the organ may be used in liturgical services, provided they are played in a manner that is suitable to public worship." This decision deliberately refrains from singling out specific instruments. Their use depends on circumstances, the nature of the congregation, etc.

Environment and Art in Catholic Worship

83. Because choir, instrumentalists and organ often function as an ensemble, they need to be located together in such a way that the organist can see the other musicians and the liturgical action directly or by means of a simple mirror . . . . Proper space must also be planned for other musical instruments used in liturgical celebrations.

Liturgical Music Today

56. The liturgy prefers song to instrumental music. "As a combina-

tion of sacred music and words it forms a necessary or integral part of the solemn liturgy." Yet the contribution of instrumentalists is also important, both in accompanying the singing and in playing by themselves.

57. Church music legislation of the past reflected a culture in which singing was not only primary, but was presumed to be unaccompanied (chant and polyphony). The music of today, as indeed musical culture today, regularly presumes that the song is accompanied. This places instruments in a different light. The song achieves much of its vitality from the rhythm and harmony of its accompaniment. Instrumental accompaniment is a great support to an assembly in learning new music and in giving full voice to its prayer and praise in worship.

58. Instrumental music can also assist the assembly in preparing for worship, in meditating on the mysteries, and in joyfully progressing in its passage from liturgy to life. Instrumental music, used in this way, must be understood as more than an easily dispensable adornment to the rites, a decoration to dress up a ceremony. It is rather ministerial, helping the assembly to rejoice, to weep, to be of one mind, to be converted, to pray. There is a large repertoire of organ music which has always been closely associated with the liturgy. Much suitable music can be selected from repertoires of other appropriate instruments as well.

59. The proper place of silence must not be neglected, and the temptation must be resisted to cover every moment with music. There are times when an instrumental interlude is able to bridge the gap between two parts of a ceremony and help to unify the liturgical action. But music's function is always ministerial and must never degenerate into idle background music.

Reflection

The psalmist's command to "praise him with the blast of the trumpet, with lyre and harp, with timbrel and dance, with strings and pipe . . ." (Psalm 150) is no longer a text only to be prayed from the psalter. It is a mandate presently observed by thousands of liturgical assemblies whose vision embraces all creation as good and recognizes that musical art in all its forms has the potential of serving God's people at prayer. Today all instruments, regardless of their past classifications into "religious" and "profane," may be admitted into Christian worship provided their use accords with the nature of the liturgical action and enhances the prayer of the assembly. As a result, instrumental ensembles of various sizes and sonorities are common not only in cathedrals and major churches but also in many parishes. Guitars are most frequently used, often in conjunction with a few percussion, wind, or string instruments. At times larger or more formal ensembles, e.g., string and brass quartets, make their own contribution. This variety of instruments, the combination of their numerous sounds, all eloquently express the legitimate diversity which exists among local communities and their styles and rhythms of celebration.

The music of the assembly is, of course, primarily sung praise which is never to be supplanted or overwhelmed by any form of instrumental music. Yet various instruments can support, energize, and beautify the singing of the people. As such they serve as an extension of the human voice. This is true not only of hymnody but also of acclamations. And just as the choir can often make its individual contribution to the celebration, so there are moments when instrumentalists may do likewise, e.g., by playing ensemble or solo selections before and after the liturgy, at the preparation of the gifts, and at other appropriate times. Moreover, the meaning and mood of certain readings may be more effectively communicated when proclaimed against a discreet instrumental setting. When employing larger or special instrumental ensembles, the rhythms of the liturgical year and the dynamics of the celebration need be considered. Using augmented instrumental resources on the Feast of the Assumption and not at the Easter Vigil, for example, does not speak well of the community's understanding of its cycle of feasts and seasons. When instruments accompany and enhance the assembly's acclamations during the eucharistic prayer, then the importance of this prayer is highlighted as the center of the whole eucharistic celebration.

The service of the instrumentalist is unquestionably unique since it is the only ministry that employs sounds rather than words. It is through nonverbal communication alone that the instrumentalist helps create an atmosphere of prayer. As a musician, the instrumentalist is a servant of art; as a minister, he or she is a servant of the community. Both enjoin more than well-intentioned efforts since "amateurism" replacing technical competence is as disastrous in the liturgical assembly as it is in the concert hall. But musical liturgy demands more than accomplished musicianship. It requires that the instrumentalist possess the ability to touch the spirit of those gathered for worship, to intone melodies of praise, hope, and expectation that truly reverberate within the hearts of God's people. When this happens, art becomes prayer, and the artist is transformed into a minister.

Suggested Questions for Discussion

1. In what ways may instrumental music serve the prayer of the assembly? Can it ever detract from this prayer?
2. How can instrumentalists be assisted to understand their role as enablers of common prayer?
3. Are there any particular instruments which better assist the song of the assembly than others?
4. What physical factors of the worship space would influence the number and types of instruments used at a particular celebration?

5. What ritual factors would influence the number and type of instruments used at a particular celebration?
6. How would the rhythms of the liturgical year influence the number and type of instruments used?
7. What are the advantages and disadvantages of recruiting instrumentalists from among the "amateur" musicians in the community?
8. Should the community ever hire paid professional instrumentalists who do not have a commitment to the Church's ministry of music?

Bibliography

Baranowski, David and Peter Harvey. "Use All Your Resources." *Pastoral Music* 3:3 (February-March 1979), pp. 9-11.

Bauman, William A. *The Ministry of Music: A Guide for the Practicing Church Musician.* 2nd edition. pp. 73-88.

Deiss, Lucien. *Persons in Liturgical Celebrations*, p. 47.

Deiss, Lucien. *Spirit and Song of the New Liturgy*, pp. 230-233.

Gelineau, Joseph. *Voices and Instruments in Christian Worship*, pp. 148-158.

Onofrey, Robert E. and James E. Froelich. "Instrumental Music: Sacred Communication." *Pastoral Music* 3:3 (February-March 1979), pp. 15-17.

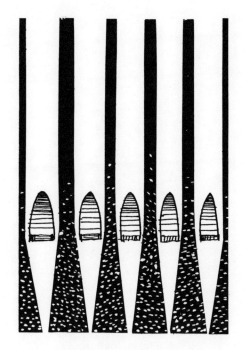

7
Organist

7

Organist

Historical Background

Although ancient folklore attributed the origin of the organ to the god Pan or to Jubal, historians can only speculate as to the beginnings of the instrument. What is certain is that the organ first appeared in the Near East where its earliest descriptions predate the Christian era. Primarily used outdoors for processions, games, and other civic functions, the instrument was also employed in certain pagan cults as a means for driving away the harmful spirits whom the ancients believed could not tolerate any noise. In fact, stridency and sheer volume of sound seem to have been its distinguishing features. If we are to believe St. Jerome (c.342-420), an organ at Jerusalem could be heard nearly a mile away at the Mount of Olives.[1]

Various miniatures and bas-reliefs show that the organ was long used for secular purposes in the West but, like other instruments, was excluded from Christian worship. Legend relates that Pope Vitalian (657-672) introduced a pneumatic organ at Rome to improve the singing of the people, yet this cannot be corroborated by any historical evidence. It was, rather, during Carolingian times and in Frankish lands that the instrument's religious associations developed. In 757 the Byzantine Emperor Copronymus VI presented an organ to Pepin. Another was received by Charlemagne from the Caliph Haroun Alrashid and installed in a church at Aix-la-Chapelle. So impressed was Charlemagne by this gift that he ordered a similar instrument to be constructed for the cathedral in the same city. The art of organ building seems to have especially flourished in Germany where Walafrid Strabo (c.808-849) explicitly mentions the organ as a church instrument.[2] Its fame spread even to Rome: Pope John VIII (872-882) requested one from the bishop of Freising. Testifying to the great interest in organ construction is a small treatise, dating from the late ninth or the tenth century, describing the measurement of organ pipes.[3] In spite of the evidence attesting to the growing interest in the instrument, we can only conjecture as to what part, if any, it played in the celebration of the liturgy. Some, however, believe that from the start the organ accompanied the singing of the sequence.[4]

Although earlier instruments were undoubtedly small, by the tenth century larger organs were being constructed. An organ at Winchester in England, according to the monk Wulstan (c.1009-1095), had twenty-six bellows and was worked by seventy strong men "laboring with their arms, covered with perspiration, each inciting his companions to drive the wind up with their strength, that the full-bosomed box may speak with its 400 pipes."[5] Yet these advances were not without their critics. St. Aelred (1109-1167), an English monk, complained: "Why such organs and so many cymbals (bells?) in the Church? What with the sound of the bellows, the noise of the cymbals and the incited strains of the organ pipes, the common folk stand with wondering faces, trembling and amazed."[6]

Despite such resistance, the organ increased in popularity. In addition to such massive instruments as that in the Amiens cathedral, which in 1429 had 2500 pipes, there were also smaller instruments. There was, for example, the portative or portable organ used for domestic purposes and perhaps processions. Also popular were smaller positive organs which were stationary. According to Bar Hebraeus (1226-1286), a Syrian bishop who traveled widely in the Orient, all the churches of the East and West had adopted the organ.[7] Yet it is more probable that the instrument became widespread in the churches of the West only toward the end of the fifteenth century.

The earliest organ compositions, which appeared only after the invention of the keyboard tablature in the fourteenth century, show that one of the important liturgical functions of the instrument was to alternate with the singers. For some time already it had been customary to alternate plainsong and polyphony in the singing of various liturgical texts. For example, the first Kyrie would be sung in unisonous plainsong, the second in polyphony, the third in plainsong, the first Christe in polyphony, etc. But as the organ became more refined and especially during the Renaissance, the organist supplanted the singers in performing the polyphonic sections of the composition. This technique was applied to certain parts of the Ordinary of the Mass, e.g., the "Organ Mass" which first appeared at the beginning of the fifteenth century, as well as to the chants of the Office, especially the Magnificat. In addition to alternating with the singers, the organist had several other functions: intoning various choir parts, whether sung in plainsong or in polyphony; accompanying the plainsong, at times even that of the priest; and in the Renaissance period, providing a chordal reinforcement for certain choral compositions and even supplying for some of their parts. Moreover, during the sixteenth and seventeenth centuries independent instrumental forms such as the ricercar, toccata, and organ hymn were cultivated and reached unparalled heights in the music of Johann Sebastian Bach (1685-1750). In Catholic worship such compositions not only encircled the liturgy but at times were even interpolated within it, e.g., between the epistle and the gospel.

From about the beginning of the eighteenth century the role of the organ attained even more prominence in the Roman liturgy. The traditional practice of alternating with the choir continued, especially in the celebration of the Hours. In this case one of the singers would pronounce aloud the texts of those psalm verses or hymn stanzas replaced by the organ.[8] At Sung Masses the playing of the organ could substitute for the singing of the gradual, offertory, and postcommunion, provided that the priest silently recited the prescribed texts.[9] And as financial considerations often prohibited the use of orchestral instruments, composers began to write choral music with organ rather than instrumental accompaniment. The role of the organist was generally governed by the flow of the ritual action during the Sung Mass and the Office. This was, however, less true for the Low Mass where, especially in France, the organist merely improvised uninterruptedly throughout the whole liturgy and thus provided a musical backdrop to inspire the silent prayers of priest and people.

Although long used in Catholic worship, the organ was not officially recognized as the liturgical instrument par excellence till the present century. During the Middle Ages the position of the Church toward the organ was more or less neutral. There were, it is true, some initial reservations, such as that of Nicholas of Cusa (c.1400-1464) who as papal legate in Germany wanted to limit its playing to the first half of the Mass,[10] but the general attitude was that of simple acceptance. Not even the Council of Trent singled out the organ for special attention. No mention is made of the instrument in the liturgical books issuing from the Tridentine reform other than in the *Caeremoniale Episcoporum*, a book first issued in 1600 which describes celebrations presided over by the bishop. Though the organ is often mentioned in eighteenth and nineteenth century Roman directives on sacred music, it is almost always in terms of reprobating such practices as the organist playing theatrical and other secular music during the liturgy. It was only in 1928 and by means of Pope Pius XI's apostolic constitution *Divini cultus sanctitatem* that the organ came to be officially honored as especially suitable for cult. After affirming the human voice as the most perfect instrument, the Pontiff went on to say: "There is one musical instrument, however, which properly and by tradition belongs to the Church, and that is the organ. On account of its grandeur and majesty it has always been considered worthy to mingle with liturgical rites, whether for accompanying the chant, or, when the choir is silent, for eliciting soft harmonies at fitting times."[11] Continuing this process of canonization was Pope Pius XII who in his *Musicae sacrae disciplina* of December 25, 1955 stated that among the instruments that have a place in the church the "organ rightly holds the principal position, since it is especially fitted for the sacred chants and sacred rites. It adds a wonderful splendor and a special magnificence to the ceremonies of the Church. It moves the souls of the faithful by the grandeur and sweetness of its tones. It gives minds an almost heavenly joy and lifts them up powerfully to God and to higher things" (n.58).[12] Certainly more restrained is the *Constitution on the Sacred Liturgy* which, aware of the differences among local Churches with their indigenous traditions of music, no longer speaks of the organ as enjoying a "principal position" but merely states that it "is to be held in high esteem, for it is . . . traditional" (n.120).

Documentation

Constitution on the Sacred Liturgy

120. In the Latin Church the pipe organ is to be held in high esteem, for it is the traditional musical instrument which adds a wonderful splendor to the Church's ceremonies and powerfully lifts up man's mind to God and to higher things.

Instruction on the Proper Implementation of the Constitution on the Sacred Liturgy

97. The places for the schola and the organ shall be so arranged that it will be clearly evident that the singers and the organist form a part of the united community of the faithful so that they may fulfill their liturgical functions more suitably.

General Instruction of the Roman Missal

63. The schola or choir exercises a liturgical function. It sings the different parts proper to it and encourages active participation of the people in singing. What is said about the schola of singers applies in a similar way to other musicians, especially the organist.

275. The organ and other approved musical instruments should be located in a suitable place so that they can assist both choir and people when they are singing and can be heard properly when played alone.

Music in Catholic Worship

37. Song is not the only kind of music suitable for liturgical celebration. Music performed on the organ and other instruments can stimulate feelings of joy and contemplation at appropriate times. This can be done effectively at the following points: an instrumental prelude, a soft background to a spoken psalm, at the preparation of the gifts in place of singing, during portions of the communion rite, and the recessional.

38. The *proper placing* of the organ according to the arrangement

and acoustics of the church will facilitate celebration. Practically speaking, the choir must be near the director and the organ (both console and sound) . . . . Locating the organ console too far from the congregation causes a time lag which tends to make the singing drag unless the organist is trained to cope with it. A location near the front pews will facilitate congregational singing.

Environment and Art in Catholic Worship

83. Because choir, instrumentalists and organ often function as an ensemble, they need to be located together in such a way that the organist can see the other musicians and the liturgical action directly or by means of a simple mirror. Organ consoles can be detached from the pipework and their connection supplied by flexible means. This allows for movable consoles, which may be an advantage, especially when the liturgical space serves other functions as well. However, self-contained organs, where console and pipework are united in a single element, are a possibility also, and can be designed so that the whole organ is movable. Organs designed for liturgical rather than concert purposes need not be very large; they should not be grandiose or visually dominating. But they should be superior musically, and as with all artifacts, the instrument and its casework should be authentic, beautiful and coherent with its environment.

Reflection

Fortunate indeed is the Christian community served by a competent and liturgically sensitive organist. Admittedly, as history teaches, no musical instrument is indispensable to the assembly's worship. Yet in most communities the ministry of the organist plays a vital and renewed role in enabling prayer among a people who have gathered for this purpose. The days of the organist impersonally grinding out innumerable Masses from a distant loft or of the instrumentalist who merely "plays a service" are now mostly memories. Today the role of the organist is that of a true pastoral musician serving as a member of the community and bringing the art of pure sound to quicken the pulse of a people alive in the Lord.

Formerly, at least in most Roman communities, the organist was the sole instrumentalist for the liturgy. Today this is no longer true since other instrumentalists are also called upon to contribute their artistry to the worship of the assembly. Nevertheless, the organ still enjoys a preeminent role, for it is a unique instrument capable of providing diverse tone colors and countless combinations of sonorities. When played by a talented musician, the organ remains unequaled in contributing to the very sound of the liturgy. It is capable of inspiring joyful praise, eliciting simple adoration, inviting prayerful reflection, and articulating the song of the heart at moments when words falter.

For this to happen the organist must have mastered the techniques of using the instrument well. Indispensable is proficiency in playing service music and hymns, in accompanying the assembly, the cantor, and the choir, and in using the organ as a solo instrument. The accomplished organist is also capable of transposing and of improvising, the latter being an art far removed from aimless meanderings at the keyboard. As a liturgical minister the organist has a feel for the innate dynamics of the celebration with its interplay of strong and weak ritual moments. He or she is attuned to the various moods and rhythms evoked by a cycle of changing feasts and seasons. Moreover, knowing when not to play is just as important as knowing when to play, since the use of the instrument for its own sake highlights the artist rather than the action of the community that is served. In particular, the organist as a minister is aware that liturgical celebrations devoid of time for silent prayer beget a prayerless people, and consequently makes scrupulous efforts to allow these precious moments of silence to happen.

More than any other musician the organist interacts with the whole assembly and its various ministers. It is the organist who often accompanies, sustains, and leads the sung prayer of the assembly. Through the use of varied harmonizations and other creative techniques of accompaniment, hymnody is rescued from the boredom that often ensues from repetition. Well-prepared introductions establish pitch and provide the assembly with a pattern for exact rhythm and proper tempo. Of no minor importance is the organist's role in accompanying the cantor and the choir. This skill, whose musical demands are so often underestimated, strengthens and enhances the effectiveness of these ministries. Before the liturgy the organist may collaborate with the ministers of hospitality by providing music that bespeaks the importance of the occasion and of the people who are gathering for it. And, depending on the nature of the feast or season, the deacon's dismissal can be extended by the sound of the organ whose strains echo the spirit of the celebration.

In an allocution delivered on the eve of the Council for the blessing of the new organ in St. Peter's Basilica, Pope John XXIII spoke of the organ as a "symbol of the life-giving breath of that spirit of the Lord that fills the world." Whether accompanying sung prayer, whether framing the whole liturgical celebration with instrumental sound or providing solo selections at appropriate moments within it, the organist is called to unite and uplift the spirit of a believing community so that its members may joyfully experience the Lord alive and present in their midst.

Suggested Questions for Discussion

1. What different moods and feelings may be evoked by the organ?
2. Does the organ deserve a privileged place among instruments used during worship?

3. What musical competencies do you consider necessary for the assembly's organist?
4. What liturgical competencies do you consider necessary for the assembly's organist?
5. How does the organist contribute to the dynamics of the assembly's liturgical prayer?
6. In what ways does the organist contribute to the ministry of others in the liturgical assembly?
7. How does the location of the organist affect this contribution?
8. Who should lead the singing of psalmody? The cantor? The organist?
9. What factors would influence the use of solo organ music at the liturgy?
10. To what extent should the organist be involved in liturgical planning?

Bibliography

Batastini, Robert J. "How the Organist Can Lead the Congregation." *Pastoral Music* 2:4 (April-May 1978), pp.16-19.

Batastini, Robert J. "Of Cockpits and Keyboards: Practical Helps for Parish Organists." *Modern Liturgy* 7:2 (March-April 1980), pp.10f.

Bauman, William A. *The Ministry of Music: A Guide for the Practicing Musician.* 2nd edition. pp.59-72.

Deiss, Lucien. *Persons in Liturgical Celebrations*, pp.45-47.

Deiss, Lucien. *Spirit and Song of the New Liturgy*, pp.227-229, 233-235.

Fitzer, Joseph. "Instrumental Music in the Liturgy." *Worship* 45:9 (November 1971), pp.539-553.

Gelineau, Joseph. *Voices and Instruments in Christian Worship*, pp.148-158, 206-211.

8

Dancer

8
Dancer

Historical Background

Rhythmic movement, one of the oldest and most universal of art forms, has long been recognized as originating in the profound human desire to discover and express life's religious meaning. Few are the ancient rituals, cults, and feasts not closely associated with the dance. This tradition, as is evident from the Old Testament, was not alien to Israel whose people danced on many occasions. Perhaps the most celebrated Old Testament dance is that performed by David before Yahweh and which occasioned Michal's reproof (2 Samuel 6:5f.). Whereas David's dance was a spontaneous and solo action, it was the communal or folk dance which was most prevalent among the Jewish people as, for example, when Miriam at the time of Israel's deliverance "took up a timbrel, and all the women followed her, dancing" (Exodus 15:20). Such group dances often marked the observances of feastdays and were incorporated into the processions of the people to the temple in Jerusalem. Among the Israelites dancing was considered a special sign of exuberant joy and as such was often contrasted with sorrow: "Joy has vanished from our hearts; our dancing has been turned into mourning" (Lamentations 5:15).

Although St. Paul encouraged the use of the body as an expression of prayer when he encouraged Christians to "pray everywhere, lifting up pure hands" (1 Timothy 2:8), there is no doubt that the early Church's judgment on dancing was both divided and cautious. It is no less certain that Christians, along with their unbaptized neighbors, engaged in dancing. The faithful were not isolated from the mores of a society, both Roman and Greek, which danced not only during cultic observances and religious feasts, but also at weddings, funerals, and victory celebrations. Although Christians did not participate in the pagan dances of their neighbors, they danced at least on some civic occasions. For instance, Eusebius (c.260-c.340) relates that, after the victory of Constantine, the Christians "in the city as well as in the country celebrated by their dances and hymns God the king of the universe and then the pious emperor."[1]

It was, however, the pagan connotations of the dance which posed a problem for the Church. Very popular among the pagans were nocturnal vigils, notorious for their ecstatic and often erotic dances, observed in honor of the various deities. To counteract these celebrations the Church substituted Christian vigils, among which were those observed on the feasts of the martyrs. But traditional practices, especially when attractive and instinctive, did not automatically disappear. They were merely transferred to the new Christian observances. It was here that pastoral opinion was divided.[2] Approving the continuation of the ancient ways was St. John Chrysostom (c.345-407) who congratulated his people: "These past days you have been received at the banquet of the holy martyrs . . . you have danced a beautiful dance."[3] In Milan, St. Ambrose (c.339-397), while rejecting the debauchery of pagan dances, admitted that "bodily dance in honor of God is to be called laudable for David danced in front of the ark."[4] When pagan influences were absent, the dance could be transformed into a noble expression of Christian joy and praise. Others, however, immediately confronted with excesses inherited from paganism, strongly objected. St. Augustine (354-430), in a sermon preached on the feast day of St. Cyprian, says that the practice of dancing on the feast of the martyr had recently been suppressed: "A few years ago the impudence of dancers invaded that very place. That place where the body of the holy martyr (Cyprian) rested was invaded by the scourge and impudence of dancers. Infamous songs were sung, and there was dancing throughout the whole night".[5] These pagan connotations of the dance were recalled by many of the early writers such as St. Caesarius of Arles (c.470-542) who, speaking of people dancing in the basilicas of the saints, complained that "even if as Christians they came to church, they leave it as pagans because the foolish practice is pagan in origin."[6]

While the judgment of the Fathers toward dance was at times negative, they had no reservations in spiritualizing the rhythmic movement of the body. Christians were to be dancers not in the flesh but in the spirit. According to St. Augustine, the faithful are to "do with their lives what dancers do with their bodies."[7] This allegorical movement of the soul was even extended to dancing with the angels in a treatise on virginity ascribed to St. Athanasius (c.296-373): "Happy is the one who fasts at that time. That person will live in the heavenly Jerusalem and will dance with the angels . . . . This is what I have written for you, most beloved sister, dancer of Christ, for the strengthening and utility of your soul."[8]

It is sometimes stated that the early Church incorporated the dance within its celebrations of the liturgy. Reference is often made to the *Acts of John*, a Greek apocryphal tract probably written under Gnostic influence during the late second century, which describes a ritual dance based on the narrative of the Last Supper.[9] Furthermore, certain fourth and fifth century heretical sects, if we are to believe the accusations of their orthodox antagonists, also engaged in rhythmic movement.[10] Nevertheless, it is problematic whether these marginal groups actually included dance movements into what we would call their liturgical observances. Nor is there any evidence that dance was officially admitted into the mainstream of the early Church's celebration of the eucharist, the sacraments, morning and evening prayer. What is certain is that at least some Christians participated in what we would designate as religious dancing. When purified of pagan intemperances, these dances were praised, at least by some of the Fathers. When the dancers gave reign to excesses or when pagan origins were apparent, even this type of dancing was repudiated.

Despite the reservation or prohibitions of the Fathers, popular religious dancing continued down to the end of the Middle Ages and even beyond in many parts of Europe. This is evident from the abundant and wide-spread ecclesiastical legislation forbidding the practice. People danced in churches, at the tombs of the dead, on solemnities of the saints, and at other festivals of the year. The practice was so entrenched that ecclesiastical authorities often threatened with excommunication persons engaging in these dances and clerics permitting them. But a few voices were more tolerant in evaluating this popular custom. For example, William of Auxerre (c.1231) explained that on certain festival days "things are done by the Church which are beyond the faith; they are not, however, against the faith." [11] By the late Middle Ages, feasts associated with Christmas (Holy Innocents, St. Stephen, Circumcision) as well as Easter had become special occasions for dancing by people and clergy alike. In some cases these were continuations of traditional folk customs. A few of the observances incorporated elements of burlesque and buffonery as on the feast of St. Nicholas when a boy was appointed as bishop, allowed to preside at Vespers, and permitted to "reign" till the feast of the Holy Innocents. But there were also other forms of religious dance which appear to be devoid of these nonsensical elements. A sixteenth century ritual from Besancon notes that on Easter "there are dances in the cloister, or if it is raining, in the middle of the nave of the church with the singing of songs contained in the processional books." [12] In the city of Puy, said to possess a relic uniquely associated with the feast of the Circumcision, the clergy were directed to dance energetically at the end of the office on this day.[13] A seventeenth century author describes a dance performed by the clerics at Chalon-sur-Saône on Pentecost evening and concludes: "There was nothing improper or indecent about this. It was done with a good intention. Yet, since the people applauded this dance ceremony of the canons, the bishop and the chapter together judged it necessary to abolish the custom."[14]

This tradition of popular religious dancing has, with at least tacit ecclesiastical approval, continued down to the present century in several locales. Echternach in Luxembourg is the scene of an annual processional dance observed in honor of St. Willibrord. To the music of flutes and violins the participants process to the shrine of the saint in a type of return dance as they move three or four steps forward and then one backward.[15] Another long-standing dance is the "seises" in Seville. On Tuesday of Holy Week, the feast of Corpus Christi, and the feast of the Immaculate Conception, ten choristers, formerly twelve, dance in parallel rows before the high altar as they play castanets and sing various songs appropriate to the feasts being celebrated. Sometimes this is done in the presence of the bishop or the Blessed Sacrament.[16] It is said that the missionary Pierre Jean De Smet (1801-1873) was so impressed with this choir of dancing boys that he instituted a similar custom among the American Indians. And as late as 1946 in the small French town of Barjol the faithful were accustomed to dance in church after Compline at the beginning of the four day festival honoring St. Marcel whose body is preserved in the town.[17]

The early decades of the twentieth century saw a revival of a more formal type of religious dancing in the United States and elsewhere. Though these initial endeavors especially flourished in non-Roman Churches, their influence was soon felt within the Roman community. Often this occurred in such non-liturgical settings as sacred dance concerts or prayer services. But with the post-Vatican II desire to admit indigenous art forms into the liturgy, missionary countries in particular began to incorporate native dance forms within the liturgy itself. As communities in other lands began to explore new forms and symbols capable of expressing the many dimensions of Christian prayer, dance has more and more frequently been incorporated at appropriate moments within the celebration of the liturgy.

Documentation

Constitution on the Sacred Liturgy

30. To promote active participation, the people should be encouraged to take part by means of acclamations, responses, psalmody, antiphons, and songs, as well as by actions, gestures, and bodily attitudes.

Environment and Art in Catholic Worship.

59. Beyond seeing what is done, because good liturgy is a ritual action, it is important that worship space allow for movement. Proces-

sions and interpretations through bodily movement (dance) can become meaningful parts of the liturgical celebration if done by truly competent persons in the manner that benefits the total liturgical action.

Reflection

In ancient mythology Apollo was considered the god of structured order, dignity, and serenity. Dionysus, on the other hand, was the god of spontaneity, abandon, and motion. Though the God of Christianity is neither Apollo nor Dionysus, the development of the Roman liturgy has been historically swayed more by the Apollonian than by the Dionysian. This is especially true for bodily movement and gesture. Admittedly the inherent need to use the human body within worship has never been suppressed, yet the free movement of Dionysus was fated to be transformed into a structured, fixed pattern. One example is the traditional procession with specific groups having appointed positions, as participants walk in a line from one determined location to another. Even the gestures of the presider underwent the influence of Apollo as they were minutely regulated and stylized by rubrical norms.

The recent introduction of gestured prayer, however, is a Dionysian proclamation that worship is more than rational order or verbal formulas. Such prayer may be very simple as when the whole assembly uplifts its hands during the Our Father or engages in easily learned gestures during the singing of acclamations or antiphons. It may be more complex as when embodied in the artful movement of one or more dancers. But in both instances it is the natural expression of a people who are bodied spirits, not divided entities composed of bodies and souls. Through expressive movement the whole person is capable of being lifted up before God and joyfully proclaiming the goodness of all creation.

The appearance of the dancer within liturgical celebration has not been without its Michals objecting to what they perceive as the sensual or erotic connotations of the dance. As history attests, this reaction is not new. And yet the experience of liturgical dance by countless communities eloquently testifies that dance, like all the arts, can be a valid and prayerful expression of Christian praise, joy, longing, and sorrow. Throughout the ages the general tradition of the Church has been to admit all forms of art, purified if necessary from less suitable elements, into its worship. Failure to do so today would betray a lack of faith in the multiplicity of God's gifts bestowed upon his people and especially upon their artists. It would also ill accord with the growing awareness of the human body as the "locus" of prayer.

For dance to be prayer, the dancer must be reverent and attentive to the common prayer of all. This is true not only of the whole community engaged in simple ritual gesture or dance but also of the soloist, one or many, who draws the assembly into the profound meaning of bodily movement. Where prayer is lacking, where the very meaning of the liturgical event is not personally experienced and communicated, then the dancer has found no true home in the liturgical assembly. But when the dancer weaves artistry into the fabric of the celebration so that the liturgy's meaning is highlighted and its dynamic is enhanced, then performance is transformed into prayer, the artist becomes minister, and the spirit of all is quickened.

Suggested Questions for Discussion

1. What is your reaction to the statement that in western culture the dance has too many secular connotations to be admitted into the liturgy?
2. When does dance become prayer? Have you ever experienced it as prayer?
3. What faith qualities are required of a liturgical dancer? What artistic competencies?
4. What types of liturgical actions are best or least suited to dance, e.g., processions, proclamations, responses, acclamations, etc.?
5. What factors should be considered in introducing liturgical dance to a community?
6. What could be some possible objections? How would you respond to them?
7. In what ways can the whole assembly express its prayer through gesture? At what times?

Bibliography

Adams, Doug. *Congregational Dancing in Christian Worship.* North Aurora, Illinois: The Sharing Company, 1977.

Adams, Doug. "Criteria in Styles of Visual Arts for Liturgy." *Worship* 54:4 (July 1980), pp.349-357.

Collins, Mary. "The Love of Learning, the Desire for God, and the Dance." *Liturgy* 19:9 (November 1974), pp.13-14.

Deiss, Lucien and Gloria G. Weyman. *Dance as Prayer.* Excerpted and revised from *Dance for the Lord.* Chicago: World Library Publications, 1979.

Deiss, Lucien and Gloria G. Weyman. *Dance for the Lord.* Cincinnati: World Library Publications, 1975.

Deitering, Carolyn. *Actions, Gestures, & Bodily Attitudes.* Saratoga, California: Resource Publications, 1980.

De Sola, Carla. "Dance and Liturgy." *Simple Gifts: A Collection of Ideas and Rites from Liturgy.* Vol. 1. Ed. by Gabe Huck. Washington, D.C.: The Liturgical Conference, 1974. pp.83-90.

De Sola, Carla. *Learning Through Dance.* New York: Paulist Press, 1974.

De Sola, Carla. *The Spirit Moves: A Handbook of Dance and Prayer.* Washington, D.C.: The Liturgical Conference, 1977.

De Sola, Carla and Carolyn Deitering. "Dance: A Liturgical Art." *Pastoral Music* 5:5 (August-September 1981), pp.17-21.

Fallon, Dennis J. And Mary Jane Wolbers, eds. *Focus on Dance X: Religion and Dance.* Reston, Virginia: The American Alliance for Health, Physical Education and Dance, 1982.

Kister, Daniel A. "Dance and Theater in Christian Worship." *Worship* 45:10 (December 1971), pp.588-598.

Matulich, Loretta. "Dance as Prayer." *American Benedictine Review* 26:4 (December 1975), pp.418-424.

Moynihan, Michael E. *Embodied Prayer.* Kansas City, Missouri: National Catholic Reporter Publishing Company. Four cassettes.

Ortegal, Adelaide. *A Dancing People.* West Lafayette, Indiana: The Center for Contemporary Celebration, 1976.

Ortegal, Adelaide. "Bringing the Whole Liturgy to Dance." *Modern Liturgy* 4:3 (March 1977), pp.8-9.

Taylor, Margaret Fisk. *A Time to Dance: Symbolic Movement in Worship.* North Aurora, Illinois: The Sharing Company, 1976.

9
Composer

9
Composer

Historical Background

"Be filled with the Spirit, speaking to one another in psalms and hymns and spiritual songs, singing and making melody in your hearts to the Lord" (Ephesians 5:18b-19). This exhortation was undoubtedly a constant theme in St. Paul's preaching since it also occurs in Colossians 3:16 and I Corinthians 14:26. From time immemorial music has been considered both the gift of the gods and an expression of the human desire to encounter the divine. Thus it is no surprise that, according to the New Testament evidence, the apostolic community was a lyrical, joyful Church because its members were convinced of their union with the Risen Lord, the Christ who rose unto a new life shared with his followers. We are told in Acts 16:25 that Paul and Silas, while praying at midnight, "were singing the praises of God." The Letter of James encourages those in good spirits to "sing a hymn" (5:13). And what some conjecture to be quotations from early Christian hymns are found in Ephesians 5:14 and I Timothy 3:16, and probably in I Timothy 6:15-16, Ephesians 1:4-14, and Colossians 1:15-20. Although details are lacking, the contours are discernible. A tradition, in part inherited from Judaism where song and music were integral to cultic life, was taking shape and would, like the faith itself, perdure to the present.

Integral to this tradition are the countless Christians who have actively contributed to the formation of the body of Christian music. During the first millenium their names generally remain anonymous. For the most part we are ignorant of their artistic backgrounds and individual achievements. We know them only through written accounts attesting that Christians constantly expressed their faith through song, especially by means of psalmody and hymnody.

Considering the Jewish patrimony of the Church, it is not surprising that the most popular form of music among the early Christians was the singing of the psalms and biblical canticles. The religious tradition, poetic beauty, and spiritual content of these inspired texts soon made them the very bedrock of Christian prayer. Eventually all Christians, but especially monks, nuns, and clergy, were encouraged to learn these prayers by heart. By the end of the third century psalmody was widespread, according to Eusebius (c.260-340) who reports that "the command to sing psalms in the name of the Lord was obeyed by everyone in every area: for the command to sing psalms is in force in all churches which are among the nations."[1]

Another popular form of early Christian music was hymnody, i.e., singing songs of praise, thanksgiving, and devotion, modeled upon the biblical texts. The earliest example of Christian hymnody with musical notation is the *Oxyrhynchus* hymn which dates from the late third century. These compositions, also used by some heterodox groups, such as the Gnostics, for propaganda purposes, became quite general in spite of certain early negative reactions against them. Among the famous authors of Christian hymns are St. Ephraem (c.306-373) in Syria and St. Gregory of Nazianzus (329-389). St. Hilary of Poitiers (c.315-367) is generally considered the father of western hymnody. Returning from exile in the East, he brought back several Greek and Syrian hymns which he translated into Latin. He also composed several hymns of his own, although most of these are now lost. Despite energetic efforts Hilary met with little success in introducing such compositions in Gaul. It was really St. Ambrose (c.339-397) who popularized hymnody in the West. Of the numerous hymns attributed to the bishop of Milan at least four are generally regarded as authentic: the *Aeterne rerum conditor*, the *Deus creator omnium*, the *Iam surgit hora tertia*, and the *Veni redemptor omnium*. In view of the popular nature of these compositions, their melodies were surely very simple, perhaps borrowed from the "folksong" of the day.

In addition to psalmody and hymnody, the jubilus or Alleluia deserves special mention. Appropriated without translation from the Hebrew, the Alleluia soon became an expression of Christian joy used in both liturgical celebrations and everyday life. St. Jerome (c.342-420) relates that "wherever you turn, the ploughman with the plough-handle in his hand sings the Alleluia . . . ."[2] We are told that it was sung by the faithful at table, by sailors at sea, and by armies as a battle cry.[3] The distinguishing feature of the Alleluia came to be its melismatic melody on one syllable, i.e., the jubilus. St. Augustine (354-430) explains the meaning of such a wordless vocalization: "He who sings a jubilus speaks no words, but it is a song of joy without words; it is the voice of a heart dissolved in joy, which tries as far as possible to express the feeling, even if it does not understand the meaning. When a man rejoices in his jubilation, he passes from some sounds which do not belong to speech and have no particular meaning, to exulting without words; so that it seems that he rejoices indeed, but that his joy is too great to put into words."[4] In the singing of the jubilus the composer and the singer become one.

As established patterns of worship, i.e., rites, began to emerge in various geographical regions of both East and West, several accompanying families of chant also developed. In the West we find the Ambrosian, the Gallican, the Mozarabic, and the Roman dialects. Ambrosian chant, which cannot be traced back to the saint whose name it bears, was indigenous to Milan and northern Italy. Only a few examples of Gallican chant, used in France and nearby areas, survive. Mozarabic or Visigothic chant was that of the Church in Spain. Roman chant, commonly called Gregorian chant, is that branch associated today with the Roman rite. Although certain stylistic similarities exist among these four groups, their precise relationships are the object of continuing scientific investigation.

The first notated manuscripts of Roman chant appeared in the ninth and tenth centuries. By means of documentary classification and analysis the monks of the Solesmes Abbey in France have attempted to restore the authentic melodic tradition of this chant. And yet the age of the tradition witnessed by the early manuscripts is not easily determined since for centuries the melodies were memorized and transmitted orally. It is very possible that the first manuscripts witness a Gallican transformation of an earlier Roman tradition. It may also be that the current Gregorian repertoire is essentially a product of the Frankish Empire. At the moment this remains a nebulous area in chant research. The origin of Gregorian chant has long been discussed. Some scholars suggest that the chant was influenced by Byzantine elements; others posit a strong Jewish background. And yet the lack of manuscripts prior to the ninth century and the difficulty in assuming that any particular musical tradition has remained stable through centuries of oral transmission leave the question unresolved.

What is more certain is that the chant at Rome, whatever its precise nature, was subjected to a strong papal influence. Various medieval sources relate that a number of fifth and sixth century popes either established monasteries at Rome for the promotion of the chant or worked on cycles of chant for the gradually expanding liturgical year.[5] A major reorganization of the chant appears to have taken place at the end of the sixth century under St. Gregory the Great (590-604).[6] Although the precise nature of Gregory's work is debated, the chant presently associated with the Roman rite came to be called "Gregorian" even though we have no evidence that any of its chants actually date from the time of Gregory.

The importance of Rome as the center of western Christianity gradually brought about a diffusion of the Roman liturgy. Imported from abroad for political and other purposes, the Roman model encountered local traditions which, for the most part, were simply overwhelmed in the end. A notable example is that of Gaul. Although some liturgical books from Rome had previously penetrated Franco-German lands, it was only during the reigns of Pepin the Short (751-768) and Charlemagne (768-814) that an official attempt was undertaken to romanize the liturgy in this region. Motivation was not only spiritual attachment to the city on the Tiber but also practical necessity. Due to earlier transplants from Rome several liturgical traditions — Gallican, Roman, and hybrid — existed side by side, often vying with one another for adherents. Only royal authority could bring order out of the confusion. Furthermore, the Carolingians, desirous of establishing a unified empire that would rival Byzantium, found in the Roman liturgy, which was renowned for its majestic dignity, a most appropriate medium for promoting political unity and attaining liturgical magnificence. For this purpose books and teachers were imported from Rome, decrees on liturgy and music were issued by synods, and the palace brought its powers of persuasion and enforcement to substitute the Roman liturgy for local traditions. Yet the change from Gallican to Roman practice did not occur without opposition. Nor did it happen without assimilation. Walafrid Strabo (808-849) remarks that the musically experienced could still hear the old tunes in the new chant.[7] In fact, a few Gallican compositions, such as the *Improperia* on Good Friday, were merely incorporated into the Roman rite. By the end of the ninth century it was the Roman liturgy which conquered most of the Carolingian Empire. The chant used — whether a refashioning of a Roman tradition or a Frankish creation to accord with the demands of the Roman rite — formed the basis for creative efforts in the appearance of the trope, sequence, and organum.

In post-Carolingian times it became customary to add a short phrase, eventually complete sentences, between particular words of a liturgical text, e.g., *Kyrie — fons bonitatis — eleison*. Although this practice, known as troping, appeared in Egypt at a much earlier period, it originated in the West during the Carolingian period, apparently as a device to facilitate memorization on the part of the singers. By adding words to the notes, singers could more easily remember florid melodies. This literary-musical form rapidly spread throughout Europe, especially in monastic circles. The trope not only offered a vehicle for expressing personal piety and local creativity but also accorded with that verbal effusiveness so characteristic of the Gallican liturgical temperament. Pure vocalization was replaced by expressive texts. This practice, which declined after the eleventh century, was finally excluded by the liturgical books issuing from the reform of the Council of Trent.

Whereas the trope never became an independent composition, this is not true for the sequence which originated by adding words to the melismatic melody at the end of the Alleluia. The sequence, greatly developed by Notker Balbulus (c.840-912) and cultivated at the monasteries of St. Martial in France and St. Gall in Switzerland, reached the high point of its development with Adam of St. Victor (d. between 1177 and 1192). The number of sequences proliferated till drastically reduced by the missal which was published after the Council of Trent.

While the trope and sequence were horizontally extending the chant's text, an expansion of the melody's tonal base was also in progress. Although certain prior writings hint at the existence of part-singing, it is a ninth century theoretical manual entitled *Musica Enchiriadis* which first details initial attempts at freeing the monophonic melodic line so characteristic of plainsong. This compositional technique, called organum, is generally believed to antedate the treatise itself, and its genesis may well be in nonliturgical singing. A chant melody, called the vox principalis, was augmented by other voices singing, note against note, in parallel fourths, fifths, or octaves. This strict parallelism of parts always occurred in the middle of a phrase or section. But at times, especially in organum at the fourth, one voice could move from a unison at the beginning of the piece and return to it at the end. The oldest major collection of pieces in organum style is the *Winchester Troper* which dates from the first half the eleventh century. In fact, it was the troped portions of the Mass and Office which were frequently sung in organum: the monophonic chant rendered by the choir alternated with troped sections sung in organum by solo voices. The melodic constrains of earlier organum, with individual voices restricted to parallel motion, soon gave way to contrary motion and eventually to many notes being sung against an extended single note.

Throughout the twelfth and thirteenth centuries the names of individual composers began to appear, e.g., Leonin and Perotin of the Notre Dame School at Paris. Their compositional style, known as the "ars antiqua," saw the establishment of complete melodic and rhythmic independence. Special attention was given to the texts of the Mass Proper rather than those of the Ordinary. Writing for three and eventually four voices, composers developed such forms as the clausula, the polyphonic conductus, and the motet (usually called the Paris motet). Whereas the clausula and the motet utilized sections of chant melodies as a cantus firmus, the motet was freely composed throughout and in the latter part of the thirteenth century even incorporated secular texts of a romantic and even lascivious nature. Musical techniques continued to advance throughout the fourteenth century, whose music is known as the "ars nova." It is from this period that the first unified setting of the Ordinary of the Mass comes, i.e., the *Messe de Notre Dame* written by the French composer Guillaume de Machaut (1304?-1377).

As composers continued to experiment and develop new forms, they attained greater musical independence from the traditional chant. Ecclesiastical opposition ensued. Jacob of Liege, for example, writing in the second quarter of the fourteenth century, lamented: "There are some who although they contrive to sing a little in the modern manner, nevertheless, they have no regard for quality; they sing too lasciviously, they multiply voices superfluously; some of them employ the hocquetus too much, breaking, cutting and dividing their voices into too many consonants; in the most inopportune places they dance, whirl and jump about on notes, howling like dogs. They bay like madmen nourished by disorderly and twisted abberations, they use a harmony alien to nature herself."[8] Similar sentiments were voiced by others.[9] Papal reaction occurred in 1324 when Pope John XXII, residing at Avignon, called attention to the centrality of the chant melodies, ordered that they be kept intact, and only reluctantly allowed figured settings by means of octaves, fifths and fourths to be used occasionally on solemn feasts at Mass and the Divine Office.[10]

Throughout the fifteenth and sixteenth centuries, the period of the Renaissance, various national styles of composition began to emerge. Belonging to the Bergundian school were Guillaume Dufay (c.1400-1474) and Giles Binchois (c.1400-1460). The Flemish school was represented by Jean Ockeghem (c.1430-1460), Jean Obrecht (1452-1505), Josquin Desprez (c.1440-1521), Heinrich Isaac (c.1450-1517), and Orlando di Lasso (c.1532-1594). Among those writing at Rome was Giovanni P. da Palestrina (c.1525-1594). At Venice were Adrian Willaert (c.1490-1562), Andrea Gabrielli (c.1510-1586), and Giovanni Gabrielli (1557-1612). Active in Germany were Jacobus Gallus Handl (1550-1586), and Hans Leo Hassler (1564-1612); in England, Thomas Tallis (c.1505-1585) and William Byrd (1543-1623); and in Spain, Cristobal Morales (c.1500-1553) and Tomas Luis de Victoria (c.1540-1611).

Composers of the Renaissance generally wrote for voices only, although instruments may have been used to double or supplant the voice parts. Unified settings for the Ordinary of the Mass, already initiated by Machaut, became common. Among popular compositional techniques were: 1) the plainsong Mass with each section based on corresponding chant material; 2) the cantus firmus Mass with all the sections based on one and the same chant melody, secular melody, or a melody written by the composer; 3) the parody Mass which borrowed its whole musical setting from pre-existing material; 4) and the freely composed Mass with all its material being original. Attention was also focused on other sung parts of the Mass. Isaac's *Choralis Constantinus*, for example, contains Propers for all the Sundays and major feasts of the year. In accord with the humanistic ideals of the period, the music was intended to make the text more understandable, to express its imagery and emotional feeling. And yet, in the end, technical developments tended to make the music more and more independent of the text.

The Council of Trent, which issued numerous dogmatic and disciplinary decrees on the liturgy, discussed music only at its concluding sessions in 1562-1563. It is believed that certain bishops wanted to suppress all music in the liturgy. According to one tradition, it was through hearing compositions of Palestrina that they altered their opinion. But it is more probable that the polyphonic music of Jacobus de Kerle (1531-1591), who composed various *Preces Speciales* for the conciliar sessions, was more influential. The Tridentine decrees, not concerned with musical details, merely directed composers to safeguard the intelligibility of the text and to avoid profane elements.[11]

The age of the Baroque (c.1600-c.1750) was one of overpowering exuberance, magnificence, and elaboration. New vocal forms as the opera, cantata, and oratorio began to appear. Of special significance was the use of the figured or thorough bass which gave bass notes only, with figures indicating the intervals and particular chords of the harmony above. The use of contrasting and blending solo, choral, and instrumental parts, already developed at Venice by Giovanni Gabrielli (1557-1612), became a hallmark of the time. In order to obtain massive sound composers extended the size of the choir: some compositions called for twelve or even more choruses of singers.

One of the most distinctive developments of the period was the emergence of two general styles of composition. The "stile antico," flowing from the tradition of the Renaissance, continued and expanded the Palestrina style with its contrapuntal techniques, even though the practice of a chant cantus firmus was gradually being abandoned. Radically departing from the old tradition was the "stile moderno" which originated with the birth of the opera but soon came to be used for religious and other music as well. Emphasis was placed on a dramatic declaration of the text, often for solo voice with a simple chordal accompaniment. The "stile antico" or more conservative approach, while incorporating elements of Venetian polychoral writing, was especially fostered at Rome by such composers as Gregorio Allegri (1582-1652), Giuseppi Pitoni (1657-1743), and Antonio Lotti (1667-1740). Some composers, e.g., Claudio Monteverdi (1567-1643) and Lodovico Grossi de Viadana (1564-1645) wrote in both idioms, at times even combining them in the same compositions. The texts of the Mass and Office were simply used as the basis for extended cantata forms with arias, duets, and choruses often interposed with instrumental interludes.

The composers of the Baroque, like those of the Renaissance, were influenced by the religious spirit of the time. They lived in an age when there existed an active spiritual life as people celebrated feasts and festivals, participated in processions, adored the eucharist, and venerated the saints. Yet the liturgy, especially the Mass and the Office, was considered as a divine drama enacted in the presence of the King of heaven; it was the religious equivalent of the opera; it was a time for appealing to the eyes (elaborate ceremonial) and to the ears (music) as the faithful meditated on the events of the past; it was a time for "performing" a complexus of rites and texts designated as the prayer of the Church. The magnificent music of the Renaissance and Baroque was born within this understanding of worship. In the words of Joseph Jungmann, "the liturgy was not only submerged under this ever-growing art but actually suppressed, so that . . . there were festive occasions which might best be described as 'church concerts with liturgical accompaniment'."[12]

Such "concerts" continued through the Classical period as composers applied orchestral techniques and structural forms to liturgical texts. Unity of expression was achieved through such forms as the fugue and the rondo. When demanded by technical reasons there was repetition of syllables, words, and phrases. Full choral sections alternated with solo or quartet parts. In brief, the devices applied to symphonic music were also operative in the liturgical compositions of the time. This was especially true of the Viennese masters Wolfgang Amadeus Mozart (1756-1791) and Franz Joseph Haydn (1732-1809). Though both wrote numerous motets, offertories, and other pieces, their Masses are the most celebrated examples of the music utilized during the liturgy celebrated at the principal churches and royal courts. Some attempts, however, were undertaken to restrict such performances and to return to a more simple form of celebration. Several composers continued to write in the idiom of the "stilo antico." Yet generally uninspired were the results of their efforts.

During the nineteenth century evolving melodic, harmonic, tonal, and other musical devices were applied to the liturgical texts. Though profound religious feeling and genuinely sincere artistry are evident in the works of many composers, more often than not the fruits of their labors were more suitable for religious rather than liturgical expression. The stylistic idiom of the opera house and concert hall were brought to the texts of the liturgy as a means of comforting, strengthening, and uplifting the listener. In the hands of more gifted composers this resulted in works imbued with a high degree of emotional or dramatic expressiveness; in other hands unabashed sentimentality flourished. As a result, dissatisfaction with the current state of liturgical composition was experienced and occasioned a search for new models and principles. Already in the early decades of the century great interest was shown in the performance and techniques of Renaissance music. In 1825 Jacques Thibaut issued a monograph on the purity of the Roman choral style. Three years later Baini's biography of Palestrina appeared. A search was initiated for Renaissance manuscripts, and collections were published. It was not long before there began to emerge reform movements which looked to the past as their source of inspiration, e.g., at Munich with Johann Kaspar Ett (1779-1867) and at Regensburg with Karl Proske (1794-1861). As early as 1830 the Italian Society of St. Caecilia was founded to promote church music reform. Yet it was the establishment of the German Caecilian Society (*Caecilianverein*) at Bamberg in 1868 by Franz Xavier Witt (1834-1888) which focused such reform efforts and was most influential in disseminating their principles not only throughout Germany but elsewhere (including the United States) as well.

The reform composers, especially those under German and Italian influence, saw as the ideal form of liturgical music whatever was written in the polyphonic style of Palestrina. Though they made no concerted attempt to exclude instruments, it was a cappella restoration which was the ultimate goal of their endeavors. A flood of music in the style of the past, much of it pedantic and stereotyped, was written for choirs large and small. The influence of the movement, while continuing well into the present century, produced little of artistic worth. The very conservative restrictions of the reform divorced its adherents from the mainstream of musical evolution and created a "church style" which was generally lifeless and musically shallow.

A further concern of the reform movement was Gregorian chant. Already in the years immediately after the Council of Trent a revision and codification of the chant books were deemed opportune. The books utilized in monasteries, cathedrals, and collegiate churches lacked uniformity. Moreover, many musicians, trained in the figured music of the day, were no longer acquainted with the art of singing plainsong. To accompany the revised liturgical books which were being published after the Council, a new edition of the chant was ordered by Pope Gregory XIII (1572-1585). In 1577 the Pope entrusted this task to G.P. da Palestrina (c.1525-1594) and Annibale Zoilo (d.1592), but the result of their research was never published. In 1614 appeared the Medicean edition of the Graduale which was essentially the work of Felice Anerio (1560-1614) and Francesco Suriano (1549-1620). Like so many musicians of the day, the editors were more conversant with the principles of polyphony than with those of plainsong. Thus they produced a corrupt edition of the chant: melismatic melodies were curtailed, neumes were adjusted to accord with the quantity of Latin syllabification. This Medicean edition was the basis for further revisions appearing at the beginning of the nineteenth century in Germany, France, and Italy. At times the 1614 edition was supplemented by newly found manuscripts, at times altered to conform with the musical presuppositions of various editors. Among the most influential of these editions was that of Franz Xavier Haberl (1840-1910). Known as the Ratisbon edition it, like so many others, was based on the musically corrupt Medicean version with all its defects. Although never juridically imposed on the whole Church, the Ratisbon book was considered official. Meanwhile at the French Abbey of Solesmes the Benedictine monks, especially Dom Joseph Pothier (1835-1923) and Dom André Mocquereau (1849-1930), were inaugurating a scientific and historical study of the chant manuscripts in order to discover by comparative analysis the earliest melodies of the chant tradition. Acrimonious was the controversy between the

Caecilian advocates of the Ratisbon edition and the defenders of the Solesmes research. It lasted will into the present century, even after the work of the Solesmes monks was used as the basis for the Vatican edition of the chant which appeared, under the aegis of Pope Pius X (1903-1914), in various books between 1905 and 1912.[13]

The labors of the reformers were officially recognized by Pope Pius X's motu proprio *Tra le sollicitudini* issued on November 22, 1903. Based on previous documents written when Pius was bishop of Mantua and then patriarch of Venice, the letter was not only the first comprehensive papal statement on liturgical music but was also a milestone on the path toward liturgical reform. Nevertheless, the letter was also a product of the time. Underlying the Pontiff's thought was a romantic nostalgia for the past coupled with an aesthetics based on transcendental objectivity. In this perspective it was the unisonous chant melody which best embodied the infinite. Thus the Pope, after enumerating holiness, beauty, and universality as qualities essential to all sacred music, goes on to say:

> These qualities are found most perfectly in Gregorian chant, which is therefore the proper chant of the Roman Church, the only chant which she has inherited from the ancient Fathers, which she has jealously kept for so many centuries . . . . For these reasons Gregorian chant has always been looked upon as the highest model of Church music, and we may with good reason establish as a general rule that the more a musical composition for use in church is like Gregorian chant in its movement, its inspiration, and its feeling, so much the more is it right and liturgical, and the more it differs from this highest model so much the less is it worthy of the house of God.[14]

And yet the aesthetic principles of abstract beauty and of seeking "the holy in the archaic"[15] were also found incarnate in the ethereal transparency of the polyphonic texture.

> The qualities (i.e., holiness, beauty, and universality) described above are also found to a high degree in music of the classical school, especially in that of the Roman school, which reached its greatest perfection in the sixteenth century under Pierluigi da Palestrina, and which even afterwards went on producing excellent liturgical compositions. The music of the classical school agrees very well with the highest model of all sacred music, namely Gregorian chant, and therefore it deserves, together with Gregorian chant, to be used in the more solemn offices of the Church . . . .[16]

Although Pius was confronted with a theatrical style so widely found in churches, he refused to proscribe categorically the compositions of later composers, certainly devout Christians who merely expressed themselves in the idioms of the time.

> The Church has always recognized and encouraged all progress in the arts, and has always admitted to the service of her functions

whatever is good and beautiful in their development during different centuries, as long as they do not offend against the laws of her liturgy. Hence more modern music may also be allowed in churches, since it has produced compositions good and serious and dignified enough to be worthy of liturgical use. Nevertheless, since modern music has become chiefly a secular art, greater care must be taken, when admitting it, that nothing profane be allowed, nothing that is reminiscent of theatrical pieces, nothing based as to its form on the style of secular compositions. Among all kinds of modern music the theatrical style that was so much in vogue during the last century, for instance, in Italy, is the one least fitted to accompany the service of the Church. This style is by nature the most unlike Gregorian chant and the music of the classical school, and therefore the least compatible with the laws of good sacred music. Moreover, the rhythm, the structure, and the convention of this style do not lend themselves well to the demands of really liturgical music.[17]

The influence exerted by Pius X's motu proprio was indeed far-reaching. Though the strength of the rigid aspects of Caecilianism gradually diminished, the influence of the movement pervaded the labors of numerous composers, especially in Germany, Italy, and the United States. The Pope's ideal of Gregorian chant as the highest model of sacred music resulted not only in fervent, though limited, efforts to popularize the singing of plainsong, but also in the emergence of neomodalism and the incorporation of Gregorian themes in both choral and organ music. But in general a multitude of techniques, idioms, and styles were employed, often joined together within the works of individual composers. Strong linear writing prevailed. Some composers, in a rapprochement with current musical trends, favored impressionistic harmonies; a few adopted more striking harmonic advances. Yet other currents were also at work which, when they eventually bore fruit at the Second Vatican Council, would profoundly alter the history of liturgical music in the present century.

Throughout the first half of the twentieth century there was a rapid growth of interest in the tradition and significance of the Church's liturgy. Though complex, the roots of this movement are often associated with the work of Dom Prosper Guéranger (1805-1878), founder of the Solesmes Abbey in France. Although Gueranger's views have often been criticized as betraying a romantic idealism coupled with erroneous historical presuppositions, there can be no doubt that his writings aroused widespread appreciation for the liturgy; they also stood in sharp contrast to the rubrical approach so common at the time. Interest was further stimulated by research into the history of liturgy undertaken by scholars at various universities and other centers. The theological underpinnings of Christian worship were being explored by Dom Odo Casel (1886-1948) at the German Abbey of Maria Laach. In Austria Pius Parsch (1884-1954) was giving a biblical foundation to liturgical renewal. The movement was provided with a strong parochial direction by Dom Lambert Beauduin (1873-1960) in Belgium. Since the pastoral goal of Beaudin and others was to bring about the engagement of the faithful in the official prayer of the Church, especially the Mass, various types of popular educational programs were initiated. Furthermore, while respecting both existing ritual structures and rubrical directives, practical efforts were undertaken to achieve the sung and spoken participation of the people in the liturgy. As mentioned in Chapter I, it was through the singing of Gregorian chant that many musicians valiantly strove to involve the community in the Mass and Office. But other approaches were also being explored. A few German composers wrote Latin settings of the Ordinary which combined part music with unison sections for the people. Some Latin unison Masses also appeared. Yet it was the use of the popular hymn within the Low Mass which was especially successful. The advantages of using a more "popular" idiom were long recognized in Germany where several composers wrote complete settings of the *Singmesse*. The practice of popular hymnody in the vernacular soon spread to other countries including the United States.

As is often the case, the experience of the people was only gradually reflected in official pronouncements. The first mention of hymn singing, and a fleeting one at that, occurred in Pope Pius XII's encyclical on the liturgy, *Mediator Dei* (November 20, 1947).[18] But the same Pope's letter on sacred music, *Musicae sacrae disciplina* (December 25, 1955), contained a panegyric acknowledging the fruits to be obtained from this popular idiom. In laudatory words never previously applied by Rome to any form of music, Pius extolled the virtues of popular hymnody.

> The tunes of these hymns . . . are memorized with almost no effort or labor. The mind grasps the words and the music. They are frequently repeated and completely understood . . . . These religious hymns bring pure and chaste joy to young people and adults during times of recreation. They give a kind of religious grandeur to their more solemn assemblies and gatherings. They bring pious joy, sweet consolation and spiritual progress to Christian families themselves. (n.37) . . . When they are sung at religious rites by a great crowd of people singing as with one voice, they are powerful in raising the minds of the faithful to higher things (n.63).[19]

Though continuing to forbid the use of vernacular hymns during sung Masses, the Pope acknowledged that

> at Masses that are not sung solemnly these hymns can be a powerful aid in keeping the faithful from attending the Holy Sacrifice like dumb and idle spectators. They can help to make the faithful accompany the sacred services both mentally and vocally and to join their own piety to the prayers of the priest. This happens when these hymns are properly adapted to the individual parts of the Mass, as We rejoice to know is being done in many parts of the Catholic world (n.65).[20]

The quest for a type of music that was immediately engaging was intensified by Vatican II's articulation of liturgy as an action of a participating people. Whereas a certain objectivity and distance marked the worship of the faithful for many centuries, the desire of the Council was that the members of the Church actually experience what it means to come together for corporate prayer. It was for pastoral and not archeological or aesthetic reasons that the liturgy was to be reformed. Nevertheless, since the tradition of the Church could not be jettisoned, the conciliar Constitution employs carefully chosen phrases to chart the future of plainsong and polyphony: chant is "specially suited to the Roman liturgy: therefore, other things being equal, it should be given pride of place in liturgical services;" other forms of sacred music, "especially polyphony, are by no means excluded from liturgical celebrations, so long as they accord with the spirit of liturgical action" (n.116). Yet it is the "religious singing of the people" which is "to be skillfully fostered, so that . . . the voices of the faithful may ring out according to the norms and requirements of the rubrics" (n.118). Composers are to "increase the treasury of music" and be mindful of writing "for the active participation of the entire assembly of the faithful" (n.121). Furthermore, the musical traditions of individual peoples are to be taken into account (n.119).

The post-Vatican II period has been characterized as one of transition and adjustment. The change from a Latin to a vernacular liturgy greatly diminished the use of chant whose ancient style, moreover, generally deters it from becoming a popular idiom. Yet plainsong, in its more simple melodic forms, continues to benefit multinational gatherings where Latin, though not a common language, serves as a linguistic focal point for various national groups. It is also true that the Gregorian tradition lives in some monasteries and on periodic occasions in a very limited number of parishes. No less restricted is the use of classical polyphony. The change of liturgical structures and understandings has greatly, though not totally, reduced the occasions for its use, since polyphony is choral song. Admittedly, the Church's heritage of music never resounded in most Sunday assemblies before the conciliar reforms, but the question remains of how to preserve this tradition. Compounding the difficulty is that much of the repertory of the Church's traditional music, as glorious as it may be, was born or developed in an age whose vision of worship was profoundly different from that espoused by Vatican II.

Regarding other forms of music, the initial post-Vatican II years were especially traumatic. Some even wondered if this was not a time of "crisis in church music."[21] In a burst of enthusiasm many well-intentioned but meagerly gifted pens produced a flood of banal texts often set to uninspired music in what came to be called the "folk" idiom. Misunderstandings between serious composers and some promoters of liturgical renewal contributed to a climate of mutual distrust. In many communities singing was restricted to the four-hymn Mass with its intrinsic lack of structural balance and ritual understanding. While many problems are today being solved, others remain.

105

For example, the arduous process of fashioning musically sensitive translations and new texts is just beginning. By and large, the search for new directions has resulted in varied compositional idioms reflecting a more general diversity of musical tastes and experiences. There is also an increasing use of music that expresses the cultural and ethnic richness of the Church in the United States. The question is no longer one of pitting one style against another but of quality within particular styles. It is sometimes suggested that a new form of music is gradually emerging, one capable of drawing on the strengths of various idioms, capable of combining various pastoral and musical insights, capable of expressing our common faith in a manner accessible to all. If not a fully present reality, for many this is at least a hopeful challenge for the future.

Documentation

Constitution on the Sacred Liturgy

114. The treasury of sacred music is to be preserved and fostered with great care.

116. The Church acknowledges Gregorian chant as specially suited to the Roman liturgy: therefore, other things being equal, it should be given pride of place in liturgical services.
But other kinds of sacred music, especially polyphony, are by no means excluded from liturgical celebrations, so long as they accord with the spirit of liturgical action, as laid down in Art. 30.

117. The typical edition of the books of Gregorian chant is to be completed; and a more critical edition is to be prepared of those books already published since the restoration by St. Pius X.
It is desirable that an edition be prepared containing simpler melodies, for use in smaller churches.

118. Religious singing by the people is to be skillfully fostered, so that in devotions and sacred exercises, as also during liturgical services, the voices of the faithful may ring out according to the norms and requirements of the rubrics.

119. In certain parts of the world, especially in mission lands, there are peoples who have their own musical traditions, and these play a great part in their religious and social life. For this reason due importance is to be attached to their music, and a suitable place is to be given to it, not only in forming their attitude towards religion, but also in adapting worship to their native genius, as indicated in Art. 39 and 40.

121. Composers, filled with the Christian spirit, should feel that their vocation is to cultivate sacred music and increase its store of treasures.

Let them produce compositions which have the qualities proper to genuine sacred music, not confining themselves to works which can be sung only by large choirs, but providing also for the needs of small choirs and for the active participation of the entire assembly of the faithful.

The texts intended to be sung must always be in conformity with Catholic doctrine; indeed they should be drawn chiefly from holy scripture and from liturgical sources.

Instruction on Music in the Liturgy

9. In selecting the kind of sacred music to be used, whether it be for the choir or for the people, the capacities of those who are to sing the music must be taken into account. No kind of sacred music is prohibited from liturgical actions by the Church as long as it corresponds to the spirit of the liturgical celebration itself and the nature of its individual parts, and does not hinder the active participation of the people.

11. It should be borne in mind that the true solemnity of liturgical worship depends less on a more ornate form of singing and a more magnificent ceremonial than on its worthy and religious celebration, which takes into account the integrity of the liturgical celebration itself, and the performance of each of its parts according to their own particular nature. To have a more ornate form of singing and a more magnificent ceremonial is at times desirable when there are resources to carry them out properly; on the other hand, it would be contrary to the true solemnity of the liturgy if this were to lead to a part of the action being omitted, changed, or improperly performed.

46. Sacred music is also very effective in fostering the devotion of the faithful in celebrations of the Word of God, and in popular devotions.

In the celebrations of the Word of God, let the Liturgy of the Word in the Mass be taken as a model. In all popular devotions the Psalms will be especially useful, and also works of sacred music drawn from both the old and the more recent heritage of sacred music, popular religious songs, and the playing of the organ, or of other instruments characteristic of a particular people.

Moreover, in these same popular devotions, and especially in celebrations of the Word of God, it is excellent to include as well some of those musical works which, although they no longer have a place in the liturgy, can nevertheless foster a religious spirit and encourage meditation on the sacred mystery.

50. In sung liturgical services in Latin:
a) Gregorian chant, as proper to the Roman liturgy, should be given pride of place, other things being equal. Its melodies, contained in the "typical" editions, should be used, to the extent that this is possible.

b) "It is also desirable that an edition be prepared containing simpler melodies, for use in smaller churches."

c) Other musical settings, written for one or more voices, be they taken from the traditional heritage or from new works, should be held in honor, encouraged and used as the occasion demands.

51. Pastors of souls, having taken into consideration pastoral usefulness and the character of their own language, should see whether parts of the heritage of sacred music, written in previous centuries for Latin texts, could also be conveniently used, not only in liturgical celebrations in Latin, but also in those performed in the vernacular. There is nothing to prevent different parts in one and the same celebration being sung in different languages.

53. New works of sacred music should conform faithfully to the principles and norms set out above. In this way they will have "the qualities proper to genuine sacred music, being within the capacities not merely of large choirs, but of smaller choirs, facilitating the participation of all the faithful."

As regards the heritage that has been handed down, those parts which correspond to the needs of the renewed liturgy should first be brought to light. Competent experts in this field must then carefully consider whether other parts can be adapted to the same needs. As for those pieces which do not correspond to the nature of the liturgy or cannot be harmonized with the pastoral celebration of the liturgy — they may be profitably transferred to popular devotions, especially to celebrations of the word of God.

55. It will be for the competent territorial authority to decide whether certain vernacular texts set to music which have been handed down from former times, can in fact be used, even though they may not conform in all details with the legitimately approved versions of the liturgical texts.

56. Among the melodies to be composed for the people's texts, those which belong to the priest and ministers are particularly important, whether they sing them alone, or whether they sing them together with the people, or whether they sing them in "dialogue" with the people. In composing these, musicians will consider whether the traditional melodies of the Latin liturgy, which are used for this purpose, can inspire the melody to be used for the same texts in the vernacular.

57. New melodies to be used by the priests and ministers must be approved by the competent territorial authority.

59. Musicians will enter on this new work with the desire to continue that tradition which has furnished the Church, in her divine worship, with a truly abundant heritage. Let them examine the works of the past, their types and characteristics, but let them also pay

careful attention to the new laws and requirements of the liturgy, so that "new forms may in some way grow organically from forms that already exist," and the new work will form a new part in the musical heritage of the Church, not unworthy of its past.

61. Adapting sacred music for those regions which possess a musical tradition of their own, especially mission areas, will require a very specialized preparation by the experts. It will be a question in fact of how to harmonize the sense of the sacred with the spirit, traditions and characteristic expressions proper to each of these peoples. Those who work in this field should have a sufficient knowledge both of the liturgy and musical tradition of the Church, and of the language, popular songs and other characteristic expressions of the people for whose benefit they are working.

Instruction on the Correct Implementation of the Constitution on the Sacred Liturgy

3c. All means should be used to promote singing by the people. New forms should be used, which are adapted to the different mentalities and to modern tastes. The Bishops' Conferences should indicate selections of songs to be used in Masses for special groups, e.g., young people or children; the words, melody and rhythm of these songs, and the instruments used for accompaniment, should correspond to the sacred character of the celebration and the place of worship.

The Church does not exclude any kind of sacred music from the liturgy. However, not every type of music, song or instrument is equally capable of stimulating prayer or expressing the mystery of Christ. Music in the celebration must serve the worship of God, and thus must have qualities of holiness and good form, be suited to the liturgical action and the nature of each of its parts, not impede the active participation of the whole assembly, but must direct the attention of mind and heart to the mystery which is celebrated.

It is the duty of the Bishops' Conferences to lay down guidelines for liturgical music, or, in the absence of general norms, the local Bishops may make these for their dioceses.

Appendix to the General Instruction for the Dioceses of the United States of America

19. No official approbation is needed for new melodies for the Lord's Prayer at Mass or for the chants, acclamations, and other song of the congregation. In accord with no. 55 of the instruction of the Congregation of Rites on music in the liturgy (March 5, 1967), the Conference of Bishops has determined that vernacular texts set to music composed in earlier periods may be used in liturgical services even though they may not conform in all details with the legitimately approved versions of liturgical texts (November, 1967). This decision

authorizes the use of choral and other music in English when the older text is not precisely the same as the official version.

Music in Catholic Worship

25. To determine the value of a given musical element in a liturgical celebration a threefold judgment must be made: musical, liturgical, and pastoral.

26. Is the music technically, aesthetically, and expressively good? This judgment is basic and primary and should be made by competent musicians. Only artistically sound music will be effective in the long run. To admit the cheap, the trite, the musical cliché often found in popular songs for the purpose of "instant liturgy" is to cheapen the liturgy, to expose it to ridicule, and to invite failure.

27. Musicians must search for and create music of quality for worship, especially the new musical settings for the new liturgical texts. They must also do the research needed to find new uses for the best of the old music. They must explore the repertory of good music used in other communions. They must find practical means of preserving and using our rich heritage of Latin chants and motets.

In the meantime, however, the words of St. Augustine should not be forgotten: "Do not allow yourselves to be offended by the imperfect while you strive for the perfect."

28. We do a disservice to musical values, however, when we confuse the judgment of music with the judgment of musical style. Style and value are two distinct judgments. Good music of new styles is finding a happy home in the celebrations of today. To chant and polyphony we have effectively added the chorale hymn, restored responsorial singing to some extent, and employed many styles of contemporary composition. Music in folk idiom is finding acceptance in eucharistic celebrations. We must judge value within each style.

"In modern times, the Church has consistently recognized and freely admitted the use of various styles of music as an aid to liturgical worship. Since the promulgation of the *Constitution on the Liturgy* and more especially since the introduction of vernacular languages into the liturgy, there has arisen a more pressing need for musical compositions in idioms that can be sung by the congregation and thus further communal participation."

76. . . . For the composer and performer alike there is an unprecedented challenge. They must enhance the liturgy with new creations of variety and richness and with those compositions from the time-honored treasury of liturgical music which can still serve today's celebrations. Like the wise householder in Matthew's Gospel, the church musician must be one "who can produce from his store both the new and the old."

78. . . . to insure that composers and publishers receive just com-

110

pensation for their work, those engaged in parish music programs and those responsible for budgets must often be reminded that it is illegal and immoral to reproduce copyrighted texts and music by any means without written permission of the copyright owner. The fact that these duplicated materials are not for sale but for private use does not alter the legal or moral situation of copying without permission.

Liturgical Music Today

49. *The Constitution on the Sacred Liturgy* sets forth the principles for the recent reform of the liturgy. At the same time it called the heritage of sacred music "a treasure of inestimable value." These purposes, while not opposed to each other, do exist in a certain tension. The restoration of active participation in the liturgy, the simplification of the rites, and the use of the vernacular have meant a massive change in the theory and practice of church music, a shift already detailed in *Music in Catholic Worship* and the present statement.

50. Some have viewed this situation with profound regret. For some, the setting aside of the Latin repertoire of past centuries has been a painful experience, and a cause of bitter alienation. "Now is the time for healing." It is also the time to make realistic assessments of what place the music of the past can still have in the liturgies of today.

51. On the eve of the Council few parishes were performing the authentic repertoire recommended by Saint Pius X in his famous *motu proprio* on music. Rather, most parishes generally used only a few of the simple chant Masses along with modern imitations of Renaissance motets and Masses. Moreover, the great music of the past was seldom the music of the ordinary parish church. Most often it was a product of the cathedrals and court chapels.

52. However, singing and playing the music of the past is a way for Catholics to stay in touch with and preserve their rich heritage. A place can be found for this music, a place which does not conflict with the assembly's role and the other demands of the rites. Such a practice no longer envisions the performance of "Masses" as set pieces, but looks more to the repertoire of motets, antiphons and anthems which can be harmonized more easily with the nature of the renewed liturgy and with its pastoral celebration.

53. At Mass that place will typically include the time during the preparation of the gifts and the period after communion. A skillful director will also be able to find suitable choral repertoire to use as a prelude to the Mass, at the end of it, and at the Glory to God. *Jubilate Deo*, the basic collection of simple Gregorian chants, should also be employed as a source for the assembly's participation.

54. Just as the great liturgical music of the past is to be remembered, cherished and used, so also the rich diversity of the cultural heritage of the many peoples of our country today must be

recognized, fostered and celebrated. The United States of America is a nation of nations, a country in which people speak many tongues, live their lives in diverse ways, celebrate events in song and music in the folkways of their cultural, ethnic and racial roots.

55. Liturgical music today must be as diverse and multi-cultural as the members of the assembly. Pastors and musicians must encourage not only the use of traditional music of other languages, but also the composition of new liturgical music appropriate to various cultures. Likewise the great musical gifts of the Hispanic, Black and other ethnic communities in the Church should enrich the whole Church in the United States in a dialogue of cultures.

Reflection

The task of creating a body of music designed to serve a community actively engaged in liturgical prayer is just beginning. This is a formidable undertaking, one that presents a unique and continuing challenge to composers of liturgical music. Unlike those masters whose names and compositions have come down to us from the past, today's composers are called to use their craft and artistry on behalf of a people who are actively participating in a liturgy whose structures have been revitalized and whose roles have been carefully delineated. There can be little doubt that recent years have seen enthusiastic efforts toward creating a repertoire which accords with the aims of liturgical renewal and which has generally made rapid strides in the attainment of artistic quality.

In a 1980 letter addressed to composers of liturgical music the Bishops' Committee on the Liturgy acknowledged the work already accomplished and articulated further demands and challenges. The Committee members first expressed appreciation on behalf of the Church in the United States to all who have been using their talents to produce musical settings befitting the requirements of the vernacular liturgy. "Your creative efforts since the Vatican Council are to be truly commended. In so many cases, your compositions reflect an awareness of the culture in which the people in this country worship. They also express your love for the liturgical prayer life of the Church with its various forms. Furthermore, the results of your service to the community confirm, once again, both the genius of the Roman Rite and the inspiration it can occasion, as witnessed through the centuries to the present day."

After commending past endeavors, the Committee proposed two working principles for the future. First, "the focus . . . in composing music is the entire assembly: the faithful with the ministers. Vocal groups and individuals, such as choirs and soloists, are part of the assembly and the preparation of music for them must be treated accordingly . . . . Composers of music for choirs and soloists must also be conscious of the need to strengthen the unity of the community and the oneness of its worship. Therefore, as the primary role of all music ministry is to support the community in prayer, so the primary focus for composers of liturgical music is the entire assembly itself." The Committee then pointed out the importance of the various texts used in liturgical celebrations. It commended composers for their growing awareness of the inspiring treasures of the scripture. And while acknowledging that not all the texts which form part of the official rites "easily lend themselves to musical composition because of their style, length, or translation," the Committee enjoined composers not to "alter the prescribed texts of the rites to accommodate the musical settings." More freedom, obviously, is enjoyed with respect to texts that are not prescribed. Yet, "even here, composers need to select texts that truly express the faith of the Church, that are theologically accurate and liturgically correct."

Since music is integral to the liturgy, not an adjunct or merely an extrinsic means of effecting solemnity, various musical parts and their functions are to be respected. Thus the letter goes on to specify that composers, in setting various texts, need to "consider carefully the genre of the text (litany, acclamation, oration, etc.) and its purpose in the rite itself." It further urges composers to direct their talents toward providing service music (e.g., acclamations in the Rite of Christian Initiation of Adults) and new hymns to meet the demands of the revised rites. Finally, the Committee expressed its gratitude not only to all composers but to all other musicians: "Without your ministry, our liturgical prayer would be the poorer; with your service, our liturgical prayer becomes even more noble."

Suggested Questions for Discussion

1. Do you believe it important to preserve within a worship setting the repertoire of liturgical music inherited from the past? If so, how can this be done?
2. Are there any models of liturgical music from the past which can inspire contemporary composers in writing for the liturgy?
3. To what extent can composers exercise their creative talents and yet serve the practical needs and abilities of the assembly?
4. If you were a music publisher how would you determine which compositions to publish?
5. Do you find that the presently published repertoire is adequate to your needs as a pastoral musician serving the assembly?
6. How can communities encourage and support the development of a varied repertoire of liturgical music?
7. What technical and artistic skills should a pastoral musician possess before attempting to write music for his or her own community's needs?

Bibliography

Bishops' Committee on the Liturgy. "Letter to Composers of Liturgical

Music." *Bishops' Committee on the Liturgy Newsletter* 16 (December 1980). Reprinted in *Pastoral Music* 5:3 (February-March 1981), pp. 2-3.

Burkley, F.J. "Post-Romanticism." *New Catholic Encyclopedia* X, pp. 127-129.

Chute, James. "Musical Grace." *Modern Liturgy* 7:2 (March-April 1980), pp. 6-7.

Doherty, A. "Music, Sacred." *New Catholic Encyclopedia* XVI, pp. 306-309.

Fellerer, Karl Gustav. *The History of Catholic Church Music.* Trans. by Francis A. Brunner. Baltimore: Helicon Press, 1961.

Foley, John. "Guidelines for Composing (and Judging) Pastoral Music." *Pastoral Music* 4:4 (April-May 1980), pp. 27-31; 4:5 (June-July 1980), pp. 45-49.

Gelineau, Joseph. *Voices and Instruments in Christian Worship*, pp. 214-220.

Haller, Reginald. "Liturgical Music." *New Catholic Encyclopedia* XVII, pp. 360-362.

Huijbers, Bernard. *The Performing Audience: Six and a Half Essays on Music and Song in Liturgy.* Second edition revised by the author with Redmond McGoldrick. Cincinnati: North American Liturgy Resources, 1974. pp. 47-83.

Longyear, R.M. "The Classical Style." *New Catholic Encyclopedia* X, pp. 121-127.

Milner, A. "The Baroque Period." *New Catholic Encyclopedia* X, pp. 118-120.

Reese, Gustav. "Polyphonic Music, 1450-1600." *New Catholic Encyclopedia* X, pp. 113-118.

Rendler, Elaine J. "Claim Your Art!" *Pastoral Music* 4:4 (April-May 1980), pp. 19-21.

Thurston, E. "Polyphonic Music: Origins to 1450." *New Catholic Encyclopedia* X, pp. 109-113.

Weakland, Rembert G. "Early Christian Music." *New Catholic Encyclopedia* X, pp. 105-106.

Weakland, Rembert G. "Monophonic Music to 1200." *New Catholic Encyclopedia* X, pp. 106-109.

Weakland, Rembert G. "Music and Liturgy in Evolution." *Crisis in Church Music?* Washington, D.C.: The Liturgical Conference, 1967, pp. 3-13.

GUIDE TO DOCUMENTATION

Constitution on the Sacred Liturgy

Promulgated on December 4, 1963, this document gives the fundamental principles enacted by the Fathers at Vatican II for the revision and renewal of the Church's liturgy. Contents: Introduction (1-4); General Principles for the Restoration and Promotion of the Sacred Liturgy (5-46); the Most Sacred Mystery of the Eucharist (47-58); the Other Sacraments and Sacramentals (59-82); the Divine Office (83-100); the Liturgical Year (102-111); Sacred Music (112-121); Sacred Art and Furnishings (122-130). An appendix concerns any possible revision of the civil calendar.

> *The Liturgy Documents: A Parish Resource*, 1-35.
> *Vatican Council II: The Conciliar and Post Conciliar Documents*, 1-37.
> *Official Catholic Teachings: Liturgy & Worship*, 197-234.
> USCC Publications Office (EC-3)

Instruction for the Proper Implementation of the Constitution on the Sacred Liturgy —"Inter Oecumenici"

An initial document, issued on September 26, 1964, by the Sacred Congregation of Rites, applying certain principles of the *Constitution on the Sacred Liturgy*. Contents: Introduction (1-8); Some General Norms (9-47); the Most Holy Mystery of the Eucharist (48-60); the Other Sacraments and the Sacramentals (61-77); the Divine Office (78-89); the Proper Construction of Churches and Altars in Order to Facilitate the Active Participation of the Faithful (90-99).

> *Vatican Council II: The Conciliar and Post Conciliar Documents*, 45-56. Partial text.
> *Official Catholic Teachings: Worship & Liturgy*, 240-255. Partial text.
> USCC Publications Office (VI-25A)

Instruction on Music in the Liturgy —"Musicam Sacram"

An instruction from the Congregation of Sacred Rites issued on March 5, 1967, which applies the general norms of the *Constitution on the Sacred Liturgy* to music. Contents: Preface (1-4); Some General Norms (5-12); Those Who Take Part in Liturgical Celebrations (13-26); Sacred Music in the Celebration of the Mass (27-36); the Singing of the Divine Office (37-41); Sacred Music in the Celebration of the Sacraments and Sacramentals, in Special Functions of the Liturgical Year, in Celebrations of the Word of God, and in Popular Devotions (42-46); the Language to be Used in Sung Liturgical Celebrations, and on Preserving the Heritage of Sacred Music (47-53); Preparing Melodies for Vernacular Texts (54-61); Sacred Instrumental Music (62-67); the Commissions Set Up for the Promotion of Sacred Music (68-69).

> *Vatican Council II: The Conciliar and Post Conciliar Documents*, 80-97.
> *Official Catholic Teachings: Liturgy & Worship*, 286-294. Partial text.
> *Papal Legislation on Sacred Music*, 547-557.
> USCC Publications Office (VI-58)

General Instruction of the Roman Missal

This is the basic document describing the manner in which the Mass is to be celebrated. The Latin text was published in 1969 with its English translation approved in 1970. Chapters: Importance and Dignity of the Eucharistic Celebration (1-6); Structure, Elements, and Parts of the Mass (7-57); Offices and Ministries in the Mass (58-73); Different Forms of Celebration (74-252); Arrangement and Decoration of Churches for the Eucharistic Celebration (253-280); Requisites for Celebrating Mass (281-312); Choice of Mass Texts (313-325); Masses and Prayers for Various Occasions, Votive Masses and Prayers, Masses for the Dead (326-341).

> Printed at front of Sacramentary.
> *General Instruction of the Roman Missal* (Liturgy Documentary Series 2). Washington, D.C.: USCC Publications Office (No. 852).
> *Selected Documentation from the New Sacramentary*, 21-87.
> *The Liturgy Documents: A Parish Resource*, 59-149.
> *Vatican Council II: The Conciliar and Post Conciliar Documents*, 154-205.

Appendix to the General Instruction for the Dioceses of the United States of America

This contains various adaptations made by the National Conference of Catholic Bishops for the dioceses of the United States as well as supplementary references of an explanatory nature. The enumeration of the Appendix corresponds to that of the sections of the General Instruction which are adapted or further explained. Contents: Introductions and Invitations (11); Singing (19); Actions and Postures (21); Entrance Song (26); Chants Between the Readings (36); General Intercessions (45); Offertory Song (50); Sign of Peace (56b); Communion Song (56i); Celebration by the Bishop (59); Women as Readers (66); Office of Deacon (127); Concelebration Mass (153); Communion Under Both Kinds (240); Materials for Fixed Altars (263); Altar Cross (270); Musical Instruments (275); Materials for Sacred Furnishings (288); Materials for Vestments, Color of Vestments (331); Funeral Mass (340).

> Printed at front of Sacramentary.
> *Selected Documentation from the New Sacramentary*, 89-98.
> *The Liturgy Documents: A Parish Resource*, 150-160.

Third Instruction on the Correct Implementation of the Constitution on the Sacred Liturgy —"Liturgicae Instaurationes"

This September 5, 1970, instruction from the Sacred Congregation for Divine Worship is intended to encourage liturgical renewal, especially according to the norms of the Roman Missal. The document contains 13 divisions: 1) the Limits of Adaptation by the Presider; 2) the Importance of the Liturgy of the Word; 3) Respect for Sung and Spoken Liturgical Texts; 4) the Eucharistic Prayer as the Prayer of the Priest; 5) the Necessity of Using Bread That Looks and Tastes Like Food; 6) Norms for Communion under Both Kinds; 7) Liturgical Ministries that Can be Fulfilled by Women; 8) Care Due the Sacred Vessels, Vestments, and Church Furnishings; 9) Celebration of the Eucharist in the Church; 10) the Arrangement of Churches so That They Conform to the Requirements of the Renewed Liturgy; 11) Guidelines for Translations; 12) Liturgical Experimentation and Adaptation; 13) Liturgical Renewal as a Concern of the Whole Church.

> *Vatican Council II: Conciliar and Post Conciliar Documents*, 209-221.
> *Official Catholic Teachings: Worship & Liturgy*, 385-397.
> USCC Publications Office (V-148)

Music and Catholic Worship

This publication (1972) issued by the Bishops' Committee on the Liturgy is a development of an earlier statement entitled "The Place of Music in Eucharistic Celebration" (1967). The document, slightly revised in 1983, contains a short theology of worship, recommendations for various ministers, norms for selecting music, etc. Contents: the Theology of Celebration (1-9); Pastoral Planning for Celebration (10-22); the Place of Music in the Celebration (23-41); General Considerations on Liturgical Structure (42-49); Application of the Principles of Celebration to Music in Eucharistic Worship (50-78); Music in Sacramental Celebrations (79-83); Conclusion (84).

> *The Liturgy Documents: A Parish Resource*, 189-213.
> USCC Publications Office (No. 857)

Environment and Art in Catholic Worship

Intended as a companion statement to the 1972 "Music and Catholic Worship," this document (1978) from the Bishops' Committee on the Liturgy provides guiding principles for the space used by the Christian assembly. After a General Introduction (1-8) it continues by considering: the Worship of God and its Requirements (9-26); the Subject of the Liturgical Action, the Church (27-38); a House for the Church's Liturgical Celebrations (63-83); Objects Used in Liturgical Celebrations (84-106). Illustrating the text are 39 black and white photos.

> *The Liturgy Documents: A Parish Resource*, 215-244.
> USCC Publications Office (V-563)

Liturgical Music Today

This 1982 document from the Bishops' Committee on the Liturgy is intended as a companion statement to the BCL's "Music in Catholic Worship" issued in 1972. It addresses subjects that the earlier text treated only briefly or not at all because of the revision of the Roman liturgical

116

books then still underway. It also takes note of developments within the last ten years. Contents: Introduction (1-5); General Principles (6-14); Music in the Eucharist (16-21); Music in the Celebration of Other Sacraments and Rites (22-33); Music in the Liturgy of the Hours (34-44); Other Matters (46-72); Conclusion (73-74).

USCC Publications Office (No. 854)

Sources

Official Catholic Teachings: Liturgy & Worship, ed. by James J. Megivern. Wilmington, North Carolina: McGrath Publishing Company, 1978.

Papal Legislation on Sacred Music: 95A.D. to 1977A.D. by Robert F. Hayburn. Collegeville: The Liturgical Press, 1979.

Selected Documentation from the New Sacramentary. Washington, D.C.: USCC Publications Office, 1974.

The Liturgy Documents: A Parish Resource, ed. by Gabe Huck. Chicago: Liturgy Training Program, 1980.

Vatican Council II: The Conciliar and Post Conciliar Documents, ed. by Austin Flannery, O.P. Northport, N.Y.: Costello Publishing Company, 1975.

NOTES

Abbreviations. PL *Patrologia Latina*
PG *Patrologia Graeca*

Chapter 1. Assembly

1. *Letters* 10.96. Translation by D.H. Tripp. In *The Study of Liturgy*, ed. by Cheslyn Jones, Geoffrey Wainwright, Edward Yarnold. (New York: Oxford University Press, 1978), p.51.

2. "And when he has concluded the prayers and thanksgivings, all the people present express their assent by saying Amen. This word Amen answers in the Hebrew language to 'so be it'." *Apologia* 1.65. *The Ante-Nicene Fathers*, ed. by Alexander Roberts and James Donaldson, 1 (New York: Charles Scribner's Sons, 1905), p.185.

3. *De anima* 9.4. PL 2:660.

4. *Epistola* 207. *The Fathers of the Church: St Basil Letters*, tr. by Sr. Agnes Clare Way, 2. (New York: Fathers of the Church Inc., 1955), pp.83-94.

5. *Itinerarium Egeriae* 24. English translation: *Egeria: Diary of a Pilgrim*, tr. and annotated by George E. Gingras, Ancient Christian Writers 38 (New York: Newman Press, 1970), p.89.

6. *Epistola* 55:18-19. PL 33:204. Translation in *The Study of Liturgy*, ed. by Cheslyn Jones and others, p.441.

7. For a comprehensive treatment of this theme confer Johannes Quasten, *Music and Worship in Pagan and Christian Antiquity*, tr. by Boniface Ramsey (Washington, D.C.: National Association of Pastoral Musicians, 1983), pp. 66-72.

8. *Homilia in psalmum* 1.2. PG 29:212.

9. *Homilia* 5.2. PG 63:486-487. Translation from Joseph Gelineau, *Voices and Instruments in Christian Worship: Principles, Laws, Applications*, tr. by Clifford Howell (Collegeville: The Liturgical Press, 1964), p.82.

10. K. Ahrens and G. Krüger, *Die sogenannte Kirchengeschichte des Zacharias Rhetor*, Scriptores Sacri et Profani, 3 (Leipzig, 1899), p.83.

11. *Didascalia CCCXVIII patrum* 8. Cited in Johannes Quasten, *Music and Worship in Pagan and Christian Antiquity*, p. 81.

12. *Epistola* 1:90. PG 78:244.

13. *Enarratio in psalmum* 1. PL 14:925.

14. Michel Andrieu, ed., *Les Ordines Romani du Haut Moyen Age*, 2 Spicilegium Sacrum

Lovaniense Etudes et Documents, 23 (Louvain: Spicilegium Sacrum Lovaniense, 1960), pp.67-108.

15. Confer Gregory's *Epistola* 9.12. PL 77:956.

16. Confer Joseph Jungmann, *The Mass of the Roman Rite: Its Origins and Development*, tr. by Francis A. Brunner, 1 (New York: Benziger Brothers, 1951), p.358, n.59.

17. *Ibid.*, pp.472-473.

18. *Ibid.*, 2, p.130.

19. *Concilium Tridentium: Diariorum*, ed. by J. Massarelli, 1 (Freiburg, 1901), p.368. Cited by Robert F. Hayburn, *Papal Legislation on Sacred Music 95A.D. to 1977A.D.* (Collegeville: The Liturgical Press, 1979), p.26.

20. Confer Joseph Jungmann, *The Mass of the Roman Rite*, 2, p.146.

21. Confer Oliver Rousseau, *The Progress of the Liturgy: An Historical Sketch from the Beginning of the Nineteenth Century to the Pontificate of Pius X*, tr. by the Benedictines of Westminster Priory (Westminster, Maryland: The Newman Press, 1951), pp.55-57.

22. Citations from Robert F. Hayburn, *Papal Legislation on Sacred Music*, pp.223-225.

23. Confer Joseph Jungmann, *Pastoral Liturgy* (New York: Herder and Herder, 1962), p.348.

24. Citation from Robert F. Hayburn, *Papal Legislation on Sacred Music*, p.338.

Chapter 2. Presider

1. Confer Joseph Jungmann, *The Mass of the Roman Rite*, 2, p.107.

2. *Ibid.*, p.289.

3. Michel Andrieu, ed., *Les Ordines Romani du Haut Moyen Age*, 2, pp.67-108.

4. The custom of the pope intoning the Sanctus was established by Pope Sixtus I according to the *Liber Pontificalis*, ed. by Louis Duchesne, 1 (Paris: E. Thorin, 1886), p.128.

5. Confer Joseph Jungmann, *The Mass of the Roman Rite*, 1, pp.207-212.

6. *Ibid.*, pp.212-233. Confer also Theodor Klauser, *A Short History of the Western Liturgy: An Account and Some Reflections*, tr. by John Halliburton (London: Oxford University Press, 1969), pp.101-108.

7. In 1831 the Sacred Congregation of Rites, reflecting a rubric which had already appeared in the *Caeremoniale Episcoporum*, stated that the Benedictus be sung after the elevation of the chalice. Confer its decree *Marsorum* n.2682 (English translation in Robert Hayburn, *Papal Legislation on Sacred Music*, p.430). The first step toward recovering the unity of the two chants occurred in 1958 when the Sacred Congregation of Rites in its *Instruction on Sacred Music* decreed that "the Sanctus and the Benedictus, if chanted in Gregorian, must be sung without a break, otherwise the Benedictus is to be sung after the Consecration" (*Ibid.*, p.363).

Chapter 3. Deacon

1. *De fuga* 24. PG 25:676.

2. *Itinerarium Egeriae* 24. English translation: *Egeria: Diary of a Pilgrim*, tr. and annotated by George E. Gingras, p.92.

3. Confer S. Corbin, *L'Eglise à la conquête de sa musique* (Paris: Gallimard, 1960), p.164.

4. *Appendix ad sancti Gregorii epistolas* 5. PL 77:1335.

5. Confer Joseph Jungmann, *The Mass of the Roman Rite*, 1, p.433, n.79.

6. J.D. Mansi, *Sacrorum Conciliorum Nova et Amplissima Collectio*, 3, p.1008.

7. *Sermo* 218.1. PL 38:1084.

8. Justin the Martyr writing at Rome in the middle of the second century states that "when the reader has ceased, the president verbally instructs, and exhorts to the imitation of these good things. Then we all rise together and pray." *Apologia* 1.67. *The Ante-Nicene Fathers*, ed. by Alexander Roberts and James Donaldson, 1 (New York: Charles Scribner's Sons, 1905), p.186.

9. One of the components of the synogogue liturgy was the *Shemone Esre Berakot* ("Eighteen Blessings") or *Tephillah* ("Prayer") consisting of three introductory blessings, twelve prayers of petition, and three concluding blessings. For two recensions of this prayer confer Lucien Deiss, *Springtime of the Liturgy*, tr. by Matthew J. O'Connell (Collegeville: The Liturgical Press, 1979), pp.9-14.

10. Confer Joseph Jungmann, *The Mass of the Roman Rite*, 1, p.333f.

11. Confer John Chrysostom's *Adversus Judaeos* 3.6. PG 48:870.

12. Confer Joseph Jungmann, *The Mass of the Roman Rite*, 2, p.436.

Chapter 4. Cantor

1. An excellent treatment of the origins of the cantor is given by Edward Foley, "The Cantor in Historical Perspective," *Worship* 56:3 (May 1982), pp.194-213.

2. St. Ambrose (339-397), for example, speaks of readers who lead the psalmody. *De excessu fratis.* PL 16:1509. Egeria, however, in her *Itinerarium* says that at Jerusalem "as soon as the people have entered, one of the priests sings a Psalm . . . . Next one of the deacons sings a Psalm . . . . whereupon a third Psalm is sung by one of the minor ministers." *Egeria: Diary of a Pilgrim*, tr. and annotated by George E. Gingras. p.92.

3. Confer Peter Wagner, *Introduction to the Gregorian Melodies: A Handbook of Plainsong.* Second edition, completely revised and enlarged, tr. by Agnes Orne and E.G.P. Wyatt (London: Plainsong and Medieval Music Society, 1907), pp.26-27.

4. H. Bruns, ed., *Canones Apostolorum et Conciliorum* (Torino: Bottega d'Erasmo, 1959), p.75.

5. *Ibid.*, p.76.

6. *Loc.cit.*

7. *Epistola* 52.5 PL 22:532.

8. Francis X. Funk, ed., *Didascalia et Constitutiones Apostolorum* 1. (Paderborn: Schoeningh, 1905). Most frequently these ministers are called psalmists (*psaltai*), e.g. 3.11.1 (p.201), 8.10.10 (p.490), 8.12.43 (p.521), 8.13.14 (p.516), 8.28.7 (p.530), etc. They are also called singers of the psalms (*psaltodoi*), e.g. 2.28.5 (p.109), 6.17.2 (p.341), and simply singers (*odoi*), e.g. 2.26.3 (p.103), 3.11.3 (p.201).

9. *Miraculorum liber* 1.76. PL 71:771.

10. Confer Johannes Quasten, *Music and Worship in Pagan and Christian Antiquity*, pp. 90-91.

11. Michel Andrieu, ed. *Les Ordines du Haut Moyen Age*, 3 Spicilegium Sacrum Lovaniense Etudes et Documents, 24 (Louvain: Spicilegium Sacrum Lovaniense, 1961), p.619. This blessing also appears in the Gelasian Sacramentary of the eighth century. Confer Leo Cunibert Mohlberg, ed., *Liber Sacramentorum Romanae Aeclesiae Ordini Anni Circuli* Rerum Ecclesiasticarum Documenta, Series Maior, Fontes IV (Rome: Casa Editrici Herder, 1968), p.117. Slightly modified, it is also found in the present rite for the ordination of deacons in conjunction with the presentation of the Book of the Gospels.

12. Michel Andrieu, ed., *Les Ordines Romani du Haut Moyen Age*, 2, p.86.

13. Confer S. Corbin, *L'Eglise à la conquête de sa musique*, p.180.

14. Confer Peter Wagner, *Introduction to the Gregorian Melodies*, p.198.

15. Confer the decree of Pope Pius VI (1774-1799) to the Hermits of St. Paul of the Lusitanian Congregation as well as the decree to the Canons Regular of the Augustinian Order in Robert F. Hayburn, *Papal Legislation on Sacred Music*, pp.111-112.

Chapter 5. Choir

1. For a study of women singing in the early Church confer Johannes Quasten, *Music and Worship in Pagan and Christian Antiquity*, pp. 75-86.

2. *Itinerarium Egeriae* 24. English translation: *Egeria: Diary of a Pilgrim*, tr. and annotated by George E. Gingras, p.90.

3. I.H. Rahmani, ed., *Testamentum Domini Nostri Jesu Christi* 2.22, 2.4, 2.11. (Mainz, 1899), pp.143, 167, 135.

4. *Expositio Antiquae Liturgiae Gallicanae*, ed. by E.C. Ratcliff, Henry Bradshaw Society, 98 (London, 1971), p.5.

5. Confer Johannes Quasten, *Music and Worship in Pagan and Christian Antiquity*. pp.90-91.

6. *Vita S. Gregorii Magni* 2.6. PL 75:90.

7. Confer S.J.P. Van Dijk, "The Urban and Papal Rites in Seventh and Eighth Century Rome," *Sacris Erudiri* 12:5 (1961), pp.411-487 (5-77).

8. Confer S.J.P. Van Dijk, "Gregory the Great Founder of the Urban Schola Cantorum," *Ephemerides Liturgicae* 77:1 (1963), pp.335-356.

9. *Historia ecclesiastica* 4.1. PL 95:199.

10. Confer Michel Andrieu, ed., *Les Ordines Romani du Haut Moyen Age*, 2, pp.67-108.

11. Canon 4. J.D. Mansi, ed., *Sacrorum Conciliorum Nova et Amplissima Collectio*, 9, p.793.

12. Translation from Robert F. Hayburn, *Papal Legislation on Sacred Music*, p.228.

Chapter 6. Instrumentalists

1. For a complete discussion of this subject confer Johannes Quasten, *Music and Worship in Pagan and Christian Antiquity*, pp.72-75.

2. E.g. St. Gregory Nazianzus, *Oratio* 5.25. PG 35:708-709.

3. Confer Johannes Quasten, *Music and Worship in Pagan and Christian Antiquity*, pp.122-123, p.127.

4. *In psalmum* 150. PG 80:1996.

5. *In Jeremiam homilia* 5.16. PG 13:319. *Selecta in psalmum* 150. PG 12:1683.

6. *In psalmum* 91. PG 23:1171.

7. *Summa Theologica* II^a II^{ae}, q.91 a.2., ad 4.

8. *Part 3, tit. 8, chapt. 4, 12.*

9. Such favourable opinions are quoted in Pope Benedict XIV's encyclical *Annus qui*. Translation in Robert J. Hayburn, *Papal Legislation on Sacred Music*, pp.97-98.

10. Canon 51. J.D. Mansi, ed., *Sacrorum Conciliorum Nova et Amplissima Collectio*, 34, p.57.

11. Confer Gerhard Krapf and Harlan McConnell, "Church Music History: Renaissance — the Reformation Tradition," in *Key Words in Church Music: Definition Essays on Concepts, Practices, and Movements of Thought in Church Music*, ed. by Carl Schalk (St. Louis: Concordia Publishing House, 1978), p.109.

12. Translation from Robert F. Haubyrn, *Papal Legislation on Sacred Music*, p.103.

13. *Ibid.*, p.229.

14. *Ibid.*, p.353.

Chapter 7. Organist

1. *Epistola* 23.1. PL 30:213.

2. Confer Karl Gustav Fellerer, *The History of Catholic Church Music*, tr. by Francis A. Brunner (Baltimore: Helicon Press, 1961), p.47.

3. Printed in Martin Gerbert, *Scriptores Ecclesiastici de Musica*, 1 (Hildesheim: Verlagsbuchhandlung, 1963). Reprinted from the 1784 edition.

4. This is the opinion of Peter Wagner, *Introduction to the Gregorian Melodies*, p.232.

5. Confer Willi Apel, *Harvard Dictionary of Music* (Cambridge: Harvard University Press, 1958), p.531.

6. Quoted by Gustave Reese, *Music in the Middle Ages* (New York: W.W. Norton & Company, 1940), pp.409-410.

7. Mentioned without reference in Joseph Gelineau, *Voices and Instruments in Christian Worship*, tr. by Clifford Howell (Collegeville: The Liturgical Press, 1964), p.152, n.310.

8. Confer the *Caeremoniale Episcoporum*, Book I, Chapter 28:6. In Robert F. Hayburn, *Papal Legislation on Sacred Music*, p.487.

9. Confer the decree *Montis Politiani* (January 10, 1852) of the Sacred Congregation of Rites. In Robert F. Hayburn, *Papal Legislation on Sacred Music*, p.437.

10. Confer O. Ursprung, *Die Katholische Kirchenmusik* (Potsdam: Akademische Verlagsgesellschaft Athenaion, 1931), p.163.

11. Translation from Robert F. Hayburn, *Papal Legislation on Sacred Music*, p.331.

12. *Ibid.*, p.353.

Chapter 8. Dancer

1. *Historia ecclesiastica* 10.9. PL 20:904.

2. Confer Johannes Quasten, *Music and Worship in Pagan and Christian Antiquity*, pp.168-177.

3. *Ad populum Antiochenum homilia* 19.1. PG 49:187.

4. *In psalmum* 118.7. PL 15:1358.

5. *Sermo* 345.6. PL 39:1415.

6. *Sermo* 265.4 found among the spuria of Augustine. PL 39:2239.

7. *Sermo* 311.7. PL 38:1416.

8. *De virginitate* 25. PG 28:282.

9. An English translation of the pertinent text is given by Marilyn Daniels, *The Dance in Christianity: A History of Religious Dance Through the Ages* (New York: Paulist Press, 1981), p.14.

10. In regard to the Meletians confer Theodoret, *Haereticarum fabularum compendium* 12. PG 83:435. Regarding the Messaliens confer Epiphanius of Salamis, *Adversus haereses* 80.8. PG 42:767.

11. *Summa de Officiis Ecclesiasticis*. Cited by L. Gougaud, "La danse dans les églises," *Revue d'histoire ecclésiastique* 15:4 (1914), p.234.

12. Confer L. Gougaud, "La danse dans les églises," p.235.

13. *Ibid.*, pp.233-234.

14. E. Martene, *De Antiquis Ecclesiae Ritibus*, 3 (Bassani, 1788), p.195.

15. For a recent account of this procession confer "Dancing Pilgrimage in Luxembourg," *Tablet* 211 (June 14, 1958), p.553.

16. A fuller description is given by Marilyn Daniels, *The Dance in Christianity*, p.24.

17. Confer Lucienne Portier, "La danse dans les églises," *Paroisse et Liturgie* 52:2 (March 1970), p.114.

Chapter 9. Composer

1. *Ad psalmum* 65.2. PG 23:647.

2. *Epistola* 46.11. PL 22:491.

3. Confer Willi Apel, *Gregorian Chant* (Bloomington: Indiana University Press, 1958), p.376.

4. *Enarratio in psalmum* 99.4. PL 37:1272.

5. For a listing of popes and attributed work confer Robert F. Hayburn, *Papal Legislation on Sacred Music*, pp.3-9. Also Willi Apel, *Gregorian Chant*, p.41.

6. The work of Gregory is treated by Peter Wagner, *Introduction to the Gregorian Melodies*, pp.168-175. Also Robert F. Hayburn, *Papal Legislation on Sacred Music*, pp.3-9. Also Willi Apel, *Gregorian Chant*, pp.48-50.

7. *De rebus ecclesiasticis* 25. PL 114:956.

8. Charles Coussemaker, ed., *Speculum Musicae.* Scriptorum de Musica Medii Aevi Novam Seriem a Gerbertina Alteram Collegit Nuncque, 2 (Paris: A. Durand), p.394. Translation from Robert F. Hayburn, *Papal Legislation on Sacred Music*, p.17.

9. E.g. John of Salisbury, *De nugis curialiam.* PL 199:402.

10. *Corpus Juris Canonici, ed. a. 1582 cum Glossa (In Aedibus Populi Romani Iussu Gregorii XIII), 1* (Leipzig, Ed. Aem. Friedberg, 1879-1881), pp.1256-1257. English translation in Robert F. Hayburn, *Papal Legislation on Sacred Music*, pp.20-21.

11. Texts given in Robert F. Hayburn, *Papal Legislation on Sacred Music*, p.27.

12. *The Mass of the Roman Rite*, 1, p.149.

13. For a complete discussion of the Medicean, Ratisbon, Solesmes, and Vatican editions of the chant books confer Robert F. Hayburn, *Papal Legislation on Sacred Music*, pp.33-67, 145-168, 169-193, 251-293.

14. *Ibid.*, pp.224-225.

15. The phrase is that of Archbishop Rembert Weakland, "Music and Liturgy in Evolution," *Crisis in Church Music?* (Washington, D.C.: The Liturgical Conference, 1967), p.11.

16. Robert F. Hayburn, *Papal Legislation on Sacred Music*, p.225.

17. *Ibid.*, pp.225-226.

18. "They are also to be commended who strive to make the liturgy even in an external way a sacred act in which all who are present may share. This can be done in more than one way, when, for instance, the whole congregation, in accordance with the rules of the liturgy, either answer the priest in an orderly and fitting manner, or sing hymns suitable to the different parts of the Mass, or do both . . . ." *Ibid.*, p.338.

19. *Ibid.*, pp.350, 353.

20. *Ibid.*, p.354.

21. Confer note 15 above. The volume is a collection of papers from a meeting conducted by the Liturgical Conference and The Church Music Association of America and held in Kansas City, Missouri, November 29-December 1, 1966.